Here are the first thirty-two bars of the slow movement of Haydn's 'Surprise' Symphony, taken from the modern score.

The 'Surprise' is one of the six symphonies which Haydn brought to London on his first visit, at the invitation of the impresario Salomon. It was called the 'Surprise' because after 15 bars of quiet music at the beginning of the slow movement, Haydn suddenly introduces a very loud chord in the 16th bar, played by the entire orchestra. Haydn said of this that 'it would make the ladies sit up!'

Haydn lived from 1732-1809, and for most of his life, worked as the conductor of a private orchestra owned by the rich and powerful Esterhazy family of Eisenstadt in Austria. The orchestra was good and well-trained, and Haydn spent most of his time rehearsing, conducting and producing musical compositions for special Esterhazy family occasions.

Haydn was a gentle, kindly man with a great sense of humour, always ready to help and advise his pupils. He was affectionately known everywhere as 'Papa Haydn'.

THE MEANING AND MAGIC OF

By Peter Gammond

With a foreword by Yehudi Menuhin

Illustrated by Peter Morter

GOLDEN PRESS
NEW YORK

CONTENTS

Published in the U.S.A. 1970 by
Golden Press, New York, N.Y., a
division of Western Publishing
Company, Inc.
First published 1968 by The Hamlyn
Publishing Group Ltd., England
© Copyright 1968 Golden Pleasure
Books Ltd.
Printed in Czechoslovakia
by Svoboda, Prague
T 2191

FRONTISPIECE:
'The musician La Barre and his Interpreters' by Robert Tournieres.

A painting by the artist Pannini, of the performance of the opera 'La Contessa dei Numii' by Leonardo Vinci, given by the Cardinal de Polignac in his palace on 26th November, 1729.

Foreword

Music does not belong to musicians. It is as free as the air we breathe and there for all to use. The trouble is that in this specialist age everyone wants to leave it to the 'expert', that is to say, this has become our main excuse ever since Music (with a capital M) was made synonymous with Piano (capital P), and from thence on meant Torture (capital T), meant scales and scales and got us further and further away from singing in the bath, whistling on a bicycle, banging on a saucepan or shaking two highly articulate bones.

We all enjoy expressing ourselves, and after a time, mere words are not enough. This is where we should start becoming musicians. We all like to yell occasionally; what is more liberating than belting out a song? We all feel like hitting something or somebody from time to time; what is more satisfying than substituting for the irritating thing or person a drum, xylophone, wood blocks or pair of cymbals? And an added advantage is that one is left with a feeling of achievement instead of guilt.

We have let ourselves become disinherited from our right to make our own music because we have been too long bullied by huge orchestras, paralysed by canned performances and dulled by the sheer volume of noise that fills our every day. It is high time we took our revenge – and a sweet one at that – by exploring for ourselves a talent that lies to greater or lesser extent in all of us, just as surely as song does in the throat of a bird.

Read this lovely book. See how different is the face of every composer in it and this should thoroughly convince you that there is no such thing as a stereotype musician. There are only you, and myself, and the music that is dormant in us all.

Go ahead and choose your instrument and see if I am not right.

YEHUDI MENUHIN
London, 1967.

Yehudi Menuhin, his son Jeremy and a pupil, Mary Eade.

Introduction

The great English poet John Dryden called music 'the science of harmonical sounds' and Samuel Johnson adopted this definition for his famous dictionary. In some ways, this is an inadequate definition for it does not emphasise sufficiently that music is one of the great arts. But it does state one truth about music very firmly; namely, that music is also a science. It is a mathematical science with strict scientific laws governing harmony and rhythm, and a great deal of accurate engineering and architecture applied to the making of instruments and the building of studios and concert halls. The study of sound – *acoustics* – is necessary before one can really begin to understand the true nature of music. Beyond the science of music is its long history, its fascinating biography, and, finally, the aesthetics of music – a critical assessment of its dramatic and emotional effect on the listener.

It is obvious that it would take a good many large volumes to cover all aspects of music very thoroughly. In this short, introductory book we mainly confine ourselves to looking at music as a science. In order to approach this in a concise and practical way we have set our sights on examining a single piece of music. At the beginning of the book we reproduce, as a musical blue-print, a few pages of a well-known orchestral score. This may seem a little like jumping in at the deep end when you are learning to swim, but at least it presents us, in a working form, with this mysterious code which we would like to decipher and gain the extra enjoyment of music that comes from knowing something about it. The score chosen is Haydn's popular Symphony No. 94 in G – best-known by its nickname of 'Surprise' symphony, a title that is explained in the piece about Haydn beneath the music. We have selected a part of the slow movement which has a very simple and memorable melody – very like a folk-song in character, a near relation of the nursery song *Baa baa black sheep* – which has interested many composers and provided the theme for many musical variations.

We are going to analyse this score as a scientist would analyse a chemical mixture. We are going to look at every detail on the printed page so that there is no symbol about which, finally, you will not know something. This will not leave us with anything like a complete knowledge of music but it will certainly give us a good grounding and will also lead us into discussing a few points that are not actually in the score. We will know a few memorable bars of music very thoroughly and that is as good a key as you will find for unlocking the door to the vast world of music and musical enjoyment that lies beyond.

To return to Dryden's definition. He calls music a 'science' but he does not use even *that* word in our modern sense, for elsewhere he defines 'science' as 'art built on principles'. Which brings us neatly round in a circle for 'art built on principles' would also make a very good definition of music.

All eyes on the conductor. A school choir in harmony.

9

Part 1

Symphony

This book takes a look at a section of a musical composition which is called a *symphony*.

The symphony is the very core of orchestral music. We talk of the 'symphony' orchestra, the 'symphony' concert and 'symphonic' music as if all orchestral music were made up of symphonies. We know this is far from the truth. The 'symphony' orchestra plays *concertos, tone-poems, overtures, suites* and many other forms of music at its concerts. Why then, should the symphony stand as a symbol of orchestral music? Partly because the perfection of the symphony coincided with the spread of public concerts and the growth of the modern orchestra; partly because the great European composers saw the symphony as a challenge to their genius and made their supreme efforts in this form. If one composer can take the credit for giving the symphony its great status it is Beethoven with his nine immortal masterpieces. As a group of works, these have never been surpassed and will probably remain the world's most popular orchestral music as long as orchestras exist to play them.

The symphony was brought to classical perfection by Franz Josef Haydn (1732-1809) but before he crystallised the form the word had many different meanings. It was first used, in a musical sense, simply to mean a part of a vocal work that was written for instruments alone – or instruments 'sounding together'. The introductory part of an opera, which we now call the overture, was originally called the *sinfonia* as were the interludes between the acts. These early sinfonias already had a formal shape with two or three sections of contrasting speeds. The well-known Rossini overtures keep more or less to this pattern.

Eventually the word sinfonia came to mean an orchestral piece of two or three contrasting sections written for the concert room. There was little to distinguish a sinfonia from pieces entitled *divertimento* or *serenade*, or from a great deal of the chamber music written during the later 18th century – except that more instruments were used. Gradually, though, the distinctions became clearer. The names *serenade* and *divertimento* came to be

used for a suite of pieces in various dance forms, and the word *sinfonia* or *symphony* for pieces less intended for dancing than for listening to, with the movements given practical names that indicated their character: the *allegro* – a lively movement; the *andante* – a slower movement; and so on. The only dance form to remain, perhaps for reasons of light relief, was the *minuet*. The third movement of nearly all the symphonies of Haydn's and Mozart's time is a minuet.

While it would be wrong, in view of all this, to say that Haydn created the symphony, he must be credited with putting it into

the positive shape and style that have made the symphony recognisable as a distinct musical form.

There can be endless variation in the shape and size of the symphony. A Haydn symphony would usually have a brief dramatic opening in a slow tempo (a survival of the symphony's operatic background when it served as overture) leading into a lively opening movement, usually marked *allegro*, in which one or more themes are expounded, developed and re-stated according to a fairly strict plan known as *sonata form*. Generally a contrasting slow movement would follow, then the minuet, and finally, to finish things off in dashing style, a quick movement, probably a *rondo*, which is simply a piece with a tune that keeps coming round and round again. Beethoven usually dropped the minuet in favour of a *scherzo* – a faster and more dramatic piece; and later composers have further adapted the symphonic form to their own tastes. Yet the basic skeleton of the classical symphony, as brought to perfection by Haydn, is discernible beneath all the flesh and clothing that later composers have put upon it – otherwise, of course, it is difficult to uphold the claim of a piece of music to belong to the honourable and dignified order of the symphony.

As the larger symphony, and the larger orchestras it demanded, evolved so did the history of musical entertainment. It may seem a rather obvious thing to say, but most composers have written their symphonies intending them to be listened to and enjoyed by as big an audience as possible. A creative artist has not fulfilled himself until his work has been read, seen or heard; until it has communicated itself to an audience and gained some measure of applause.

A concert is defined in the dictionary as a 'public performance of a set programme to which an audience is admitted by payment'. Before the days when a public performance was supported by a population able to appreciate music, orchestral music had been a luxury available only to the aristocratic and the rich. We know how a composer like Haydn was employed by a noble household to run its private orchestra and to compose music for special occasions. Today, this kind of patronage has almost died out and music is supported by public funds or commercial enterprises who specialise in promoting concerts.

Some of the first concerts covered by the above definition were held in London in the 1670s. The 18th century saw the growth of this enterprise and the formation of societies to promote concerts such as the Academy of Antient Music founded in 1710 and the Professional Concerts started in 1785. There were early promoters like Salomon who brought Haydn to England to conduct a series of his own symphonies, especially written in London for the occasion. One of the most important London concert halls of the 18th century was the Hanover Square Rooms which was opened in 1775. The last concert was given there, nearly one hundred years later, in 1874. The acoustics were said to be excellent.

Other cities like Paris and Vienna were close behind in the promotion of public concerts and each had many societies and halls by the end of the 18th century.

Today the most familiar setting for music is the big concert hall; the orchestra, with their celebrated conductor in front of them, splendidly arrayed in bow-ties and 'tails', a well-dressed audience listening with polite attention and dutifully applauding in the right places. This setting seems so correct and established that it is perhaps a little bold to doubt whether this is, after all, the best way to listen to and enjoy music. Is it perhaps all a little artificial? Could the musicians not be a little more comfortable and at ease? Need some conductors be quite so demonstrative?

Perhaps you would rather sit in an easy chair when you are listening to music. Is the sound as good as it might be in the hall – and do the coughs and sneezes help?

In spite of all its disadvantages, in spite of the home attractions of the gramophone and TV, in spite of our having to travel to the concert and the considerable expense of concert going, there is nothing to surpass the atmosphere of a live concert nor the real enjoyment to be got out of a good one. Music and musical prowess lay themselves open to judgment. We, the audience, are asked to be the judges. There is a great feeling of togetherness in concert audiences and a friendly appreciation of what is done for us on the platform. We probably applaud over-generously most of the time. But no real harm is done by this.

The modern 'symphony' concert might be said to have reached a peak of perfection; performance, organisation and setting could hardly be improved upon in a big modern hall like London's Royal Festival Hall and other new buildings in Europe especially designed for hearing the orchestra at its best. It has not been like this for long. We have only to think of the other big rival establishment in London – the Royal Albert Hall – to recall the old-fashioned discomfort of the seats, the inconvenience of the entrances and the stairs and the well-known echo in the hall itself, which has been greatly diminished by clever modern technicians. One of Sir Thomas Beecham's best quips concerned that famous echo. 'Every young composer should have his new works first played in the Albert Hall,' said Sir Thomas, 'then he will be certain of hearing them at least twice.' Of course, the Victorians, who built the Albert Hall, liked performances of choral works by a choir of hundreds. In those days it probably did not seem so vast and impractical.

Hanover Square Concert Rooms, London. Opened in 1775, this was one of the earliest concert halls in London.

Part 2

The Elements
of Music

Instruments which are hit, plucked and blown.

What would be the first impression of the Haydn *score* to someone who knew absolutely nothing about music? He would probably see it simply as a mass of dots and circles (more of these than anything else) and a few other mysterious signs scattered about on a regularly arranged series of five lines. But even the most unmusical adventurer would perceive that there was a certain symmetry, an apparent order and logic, about the way everything was arranged. A page of music has a purposeful look about it.

Music is an arrangement of sounds. Any sound is made by causing the air to move in concentric waves, as the water in a

pond moves when a stone is thrown into it. These ripples are picked up by our ears and identified by our brains.

Not all sounds are useful to music. The sounds best used for musical creation are well-defined, clear and pleasant. Various instruments have been invented to produce such sounds. They produce them by creating vibrations within themselves, either by being hit, or plucked or blown, and then they transmit these sounds to the air. Their scientific structure ensures that the sound is forced out in a concentrated and clear way and that it can be varied in *pitch* (high or low in the scale), intensity and duration.

High notes are the sound of fast vibrations being set in motion in the air; low notes are the sound of slow vibrations. There is a wide range of sound between the lowest note the ear can hear and the highest. There are also sounds beyond the ear's capacity to hear but, of course, these are not the concern of music.

All music and harmony is based on the proven scientific fact that the notes we use in a musical *scale* have fixed rates of vibration which are mathematically related to one another. The note A (above middle C) is the result of a vibration of 440 times per second; it is said to have a *frequency* of 440. Another note vibrating 880 times per second would sound in complete *harmony* with this first note because the sound waves would fall neatly between each other. Unfortunately for us, all the notes do not have simple frequencies, nor do they bear a simple relation to one another – the frequency of middle C, for example, is 261.6256 while D is 293.6648. When a piano is tuned the tuner is making sure that each string is vibrating at the correct rate. He will generally do this by ear, letting his senses tell him what is wrong rather than relying on a scientific instrument.

Some people are good at this sort of thing. They have what is called a musical ear. Some people have so sensitive an ear that they can sing any note asked for, judging it intuitively by its frequency – this is called having *perfect pitch*.

A musician learns how to produce the required notes on his chosen instrument. A composer then tells him what notes to play. The composer's written music is the musician's guide. How does he interpret it? This is the secret that we must discover before we can understand music.

CLAUDIO MONTEVERDI (1567-1643) *Italy*
Opera began in Italy – probably in the city of Florence – at the end of the 16th century. However, the first operas were very simple and rather unexciting entertainments by modern standards. One of the first works that sounded anything like a modern opera, with a dramatic story told in song and the music being used to create the right mood, was Monteverdi's *Orfeo* produced in Mantua in 1607. Monteverdi wrote many more operas, nine volumes of madrigals and a great deal of church music. From 1613 he worked at St. Mark's in Venice, being Master of Music in the Venetian republic.

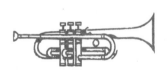
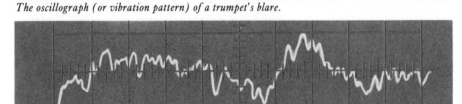

The oscillograph (or vibration pattern) of a trumpet's blare.

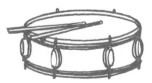

The irregular wave pattern of a drumbeat.

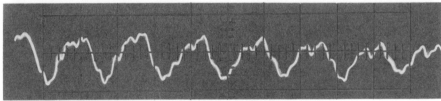

Although the violin note shows a jagged trace, the sound is not jerky.

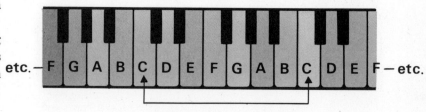

When we explain music we generally do it by means of the *piano keyboard*. On the piano keyboard a great deal of musical theory is there plainly for everyone to see. It is not so obvious on a *wind* or a *string* instrument.

Look at the piano keyboard and you will see that it has a recurring pattern of black and white keys. This helps us to find the notes very easily. The note called A is always on the white key between the second and third black notes in the group of three:

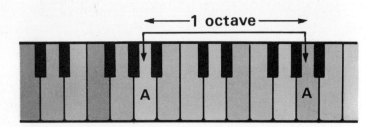

On the average keyboard there will be eight A's in all. Take the one that is more or less in the middle. There is an A above it and an A below it (we think of the notes to the right being 'above' or higher, the notes to the left being 'below' or lower). These A's are an *octave* higher or lower than our original A. They are similar in character, and sound like the same note, except that they are higher or lower in *pitch*, vibrating twice as fast in the case of the higher note, half as fast in the case of the lower one. The word *octave* is from the Italian word meaning eight. One A is eight white notes away from the next. When we count notes in this way we always include the one we start on. If you can play one A with the thumb of your right hand and another A higher up with the little finger of the same hand your hand can stretch, or play, an octave. It is a great advantage to a pianist to be able to stretch even more than this and reach over ten or eleven notes. The space or interval between an A and the C beyond the A above it is a *tenth*.

Between the two A's the white notes follow in alphabetical order A.B.C.D.E.F.G., then on again up the keyboard A.B.C.D. E.F.G. and so on. Knowing where A is you can now easily find C. It is the note just before the group of two black notes. If you play the white notes from C to C you are playing a *scale*. (p. 29)

The scale from C to C on the white notes is a major scale.

etc.— F G A B C D E F G A B C D E F — etc.

Scale of C i.e. C to C

What names are given to the black notes on the piano? If you move from any note to the note next to it (whether it is a white or a black note) you have moved through half a tone or a *semitone*. If you move from A to one of the black notes either side of it you have moved through a semitone. If you move upwards a semitone you have *sharpened* the note. Therefore the black note above A is A sharp (usually written as A♯) ♯ being the sign for a sharp.

If you move to the black note below A you have *flattened* the note so this black note is A flat (usually written A♭) ♭ being the sign for a flat.

Any note immediately below another is the *flat* of that note (whether it is a white or black); any note above is a *sharp*. B sharp, for instance, would be the same note as C, because there is no black note immediately above B. Similarly, you will be able to work out that the black note we call A sharp could also be called B flat. Its name depends on what *key* (p. 30) we are playing in.

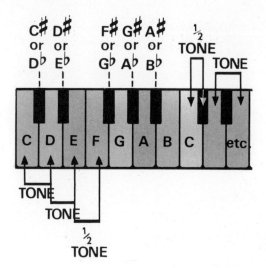

If moving to the next note is a move of half a tone, then obviously skipping a note and moving to the next-but-one note is a move of one *whole* tone, e.g. A to B, C to D or B to C sharp. (Work those out on the piano, especially that last one.) The ability to think of the distance between one note and the next, called the *interval* between them, in terms of semitones and multiples of these will help when we come to consider scales and keys.

Now we know what all the notes on the piano keyboard are called, we must find out how to write each of them in musical *notation* so that we will know which note or notes the composer wants us to play.

Music is written on sets of five lines called the *stave*. We know what the name of the note is according to where it is placed, either on the lines of the stave or in the spaces between the lines.

Instruments which generally play only one note at a time need only one set of five lines. If they are high notes they play on a stave with this sign in front of it:

This is the *treble clef* sign. In the score we can see that the violin's part is written in the treble clef:

If an instrument plays mainly low notes, its music is written in the *bass clef*. This is the bass clef sign:

The double-bass's part in the score is written in the bass clef:

HENRY PURCELL (1659-1695) *England*
Purcell was the greatest English composer of his day and one of the most original that his country has ever known. Unfortunately the British have always tended to admire foreign composers more than their own and, until quite recent times, Purcell's music was forgotten while the works of visiting composers like Handel, Haydn and Mendelssohn were much admired. Modern composers like Benjamin Britten and Michael Tippett came to realise how good Purcell was at setting words to music and, using him as a model, have helped to make his works known again. Purcell's masterpiece is the opera *Dido and Aeneas* written in 1689.

The right hand spans an octave on the keyboard of the piano (middle C to the C above).

G = 𝒢 𝒢 𝒢 = 𝄞

F = F F ꓭ = 𝄢

Through the stages shown here the letters G and F have evolved into the treble and bass clef signs we know today.

The distinction between treble clef and bass clef is important because the notes A,B,C, etc., do not occupy the same position on or between the stave lines in each case.

The treble clef is also called the *G clef* because it covers a range of notes that centre around the G above middle C – a range suitable for high voices and instruments. The bass or *F clef* centres around the F below middle C and covers a range suitable for low voices and instruments. (Oddly, its symbol 𝄢, which looks so much like a reversed C, is a sign which gradually evolved from something that originally looked more like an F than it does now.) Between these two clefs there is the *alto* or *C clef* based on middle C which is now only used for instruments like the viola and cello which have a medium range. Its use involves learning another set of note positions, which we may not worry too much about for the moment.

A pivotal or central part of each of the symbols used for these clefs in fact falls on the line of the stave from which each clef takes its name:

Position of notes different in each clef

An instrument like the piano needs two staves at a time on which to write all the notes which are played by both the right hand and left hand. The right hand plays mainly in the treble clef, the left hand in the bass clef. As we have to read two differently positioned sets of notes for each hand this may seem an unnecessary and somewhat alarming complication, but it is something that has to be accepted and we soon get used to it.

Now let us relate some of the notes on the piano to the notes in the music.

The position of the hands on the piano keyboard: the right hand plays the treble and the left hand plays the bass notes.

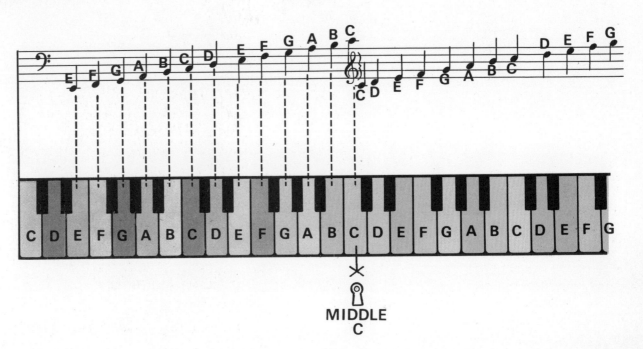

MIDDLE
C

You will notice that the C in the middle – logically known as *middle C* as it lies at or near the middle of the keyboard – is common to both *clefs*. This, for your interest, explains why the notes in the two clefs have different positions. At one time, the music was written on one big stave with 11 lines. This was confusing and did not make clear which notes were for the left and which for the right hand. So the middle line was dropped out, leaving C suspended in mid-air as it were.

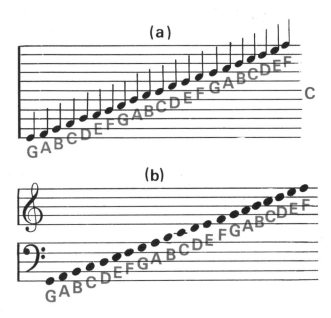

JOHANN SEBASTIAN BACH (1685-1750) *Germany*
Bach was an organist and choirmaster for most of his life, and much of his music was written as a part of his regular duties. For the church he wrote hundreds of cantatas, and three other great choral works, the *St. John Passion*, the *St. Matthew Passion* and the Mass in B minor. He also wrote a large volume of music for the organ, the harpsichord, violin and cello, and a set of pieces known as the *Brandenburg Concertos*. His favourite kind of music was the fugue, the most perfect form of counterpoint (see p. 33), and his Forty-eight Preludes and Fugues are among his greatest works. Bach had twenty children, and two of his sons, Johann Christian and Carl Philipp Emanuel, also became famous composers.

These are instruments which are grouped together at different pitches (high, medium and low).
High pitch (about the same range as a soprano voice):
1. Violin 2. Flute 3. Oboe 4. Trumpet

Low pitch:
1. Double-bass 2. Trombone 3. Bassoon
4. Tuba

Medium pitch:
1. Clarinet 2. Tenor Saxophone 3. French Horn
4. Cello

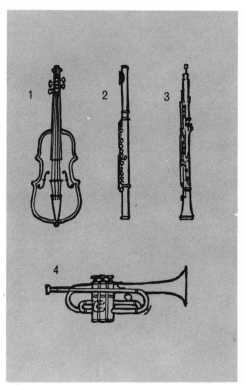

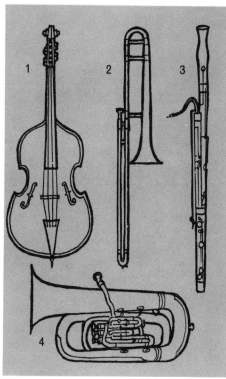

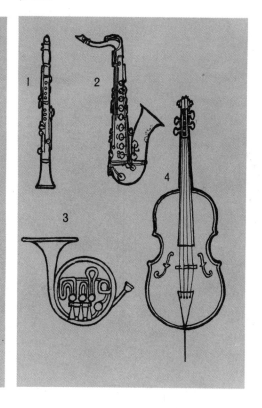

Counting the beats. A young drummer keeps his eyes on the score.

The five lines of the stave do not, in fact, give room to write many notes. The complete range of notes on the lines and spaces in the bass and treble clef staves are:

If we want to write some more notes up above these we can add extra lines. These are called *ledger* lines and are now written in an abbreviated form large enough to accommodate one note (a)

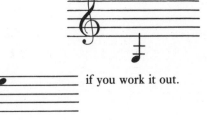

If we want to go higher still we don't just keep on adding lines but we can put a sign over them – 8vo (remember the 8) – which simply means play these notes an octave higher than they are written (b).

Also, if we want to go below the stave, to middle C or lower, then we can add ledger lines beneath the stave. This is more sensible than writing some of the right hand music in the bass clef, although obviously this note

is the same as ⎯⎯⎯ if you work it out.

The same procedures apply, of course, to the bass clef.

An illuminated music manuscript of early medieval times. Painted by hand with elaborately decorated side panel and capital letter, a page like this would take weeks to perfect.

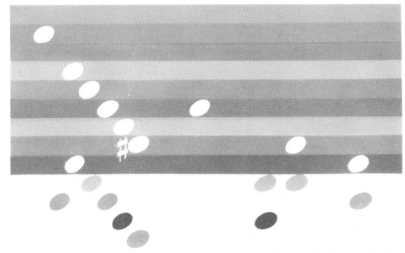

An artist's representation in colour of the music below. Each band of colour represents a note on the coloured keyboard of the piano on pp. 14 and 15.

Here are a few bars of music for the piano showing what the final result looks like:

You should now be able to pick out our tune taken from the Haydn score on the piano as follows:

GEORGE FRIDERIC HANDEL (1685-1759) *Germany*
Although a German and living at the same time as Bach, Handel worked on entirely different lines. His main interest was opera and he modelled his style on the early Italian masters. Most of his life was spent in England and he was so admired and copied, both in his lifetime and for well over a century after his death, that English born composers were almost forgotten. Sir Arthur Sullivan (1842-1900) was still obviously inspired a great deal by Handel's music. Handel's great choral work was *Messiah* which is still performed hundreds of times every year; while his best known orchestral works are *Music for the Royal Fireworks* and the *Water Music*.

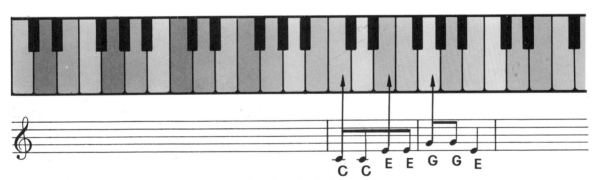

C C E E G G E

If you liked you could play it further down the piano in the bass clef

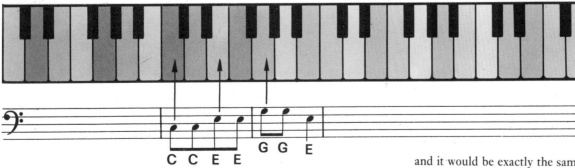

C C E E G G E

and it would be exactly the same melody but pitched lower.

A piano arrangement of the first 32 bars of the slow movement of Haydn's 'Surprise' Symphony.

Length of Notes

On the opposite page we have taken the first 32 bars of the slow movement of the Haydn symphony and written them out in a simple way so that they can be played on the piano. For the moment it is easier to look at the music like this than to look at the whole score.

Let us look at this piano version and see what we have already learned about it. We know what 𝄞 means and what 𝄢 means. Right at the beginning of the stave, the sets of five lines have a vertical line tying them together in pairs; and they are tied together this way right through the piano piece. This is simply to indicate that these two sets of lines are played at the same time. In the full score you will see that a bigger line joins the bars of music indicating a larger number of lines being played together.

Next we know the notes and, according to which line or space they fall on, we know their names and their pitch – a word which simply means how high or low in the scale of sounds they are. We can easily see whether a note is higher or lower than the one next to it by its relative position on the stave.

The next thing we want to know about a note is how long it lasts – its duration in relation to other notes. We must know this, as well as its pitch, before we can join it with other notes to make a tune.

The longest note we can have is what the Americans very logically call the *whole note*. The traditional Italian name for it is *semibreve*. The duration of this note is not always the same. If we are playing a piece of music at a slow speed it will last longer than if we are playing at a fast speed. What is important is its relation to other notes, and the fact that all the other kinds of notes are exact divisions of this whole note: a half, a quarter, an eighth, and so on.

The whole note or semibreve is written

Exactly half of the value or length of a semibreve is a *minim* or *half-note*.

If we were playing rather slowly and our semibreve took up four seconds, then our minim would last for two seconds. The half-note or minim is written

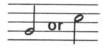

Half the value of a minim is a *crotchet* or *quarter-note*. By the same reckoning this would last for one second.

The quarter-note or crotchet is written

And so we go on dividing: half of the length of a crotchet is the *quaver* or *eighth-note*, written

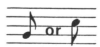

Half of a quaver is a *semi-quaver* or sixteenth note, written

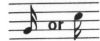

Half a semi-quaver is a *demi-semi-quaver* or thirty-second note, written

Each kind of note has an equivalent rest. This is the sign that you put when you want no note to be played – in other words you want silence for the amount of time that would be represented by one or other of those notes. The equivalent rests are as follows:

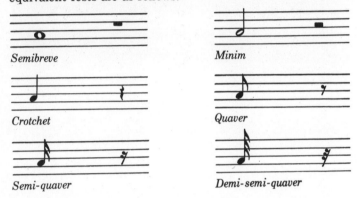

To get these note values quite clear look at them like this. In duration:

One semibreve ◯ equals 2 minims ♩ or 4 crotchets ♩♩♩♩ or 8 quavers ♪♪♪♪♪♪♪♪ (more usually written ♫♫ ♫♫) or 16 semi-quavers (written ♬♬ ♬♬ ♬♬ ♬♬) or 32 demi-semi-quavers (written ♬♬ etc.)

Dotted Notes

To get more variety into our melodic rhythms we can split up the notes a little more by using dotted notes. A dot after a note makes it half as long again.

It takes this extra time from the note following it so that four plain crotchets thus

become like this

when one of them is dotted

Triplets

This is a device that allows you to play three notes where there would usually be only two. Four quavers would be changed (by putting a triplet in place of two of them) from this

to this

Graph showing duration of notes.

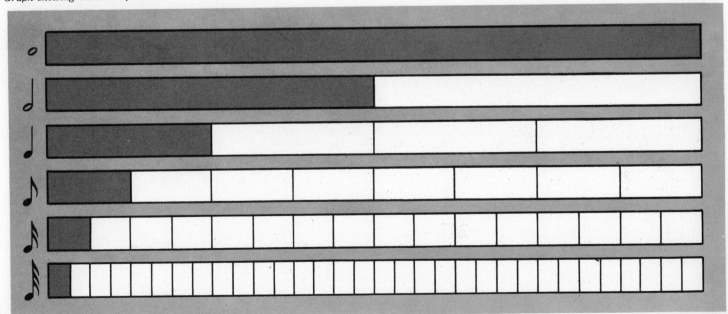

Rhythm

Rhythm is the regular beat that is in all music. It must not be confused with *tempo* or time which is the speed of the music.

In our examples concerning the duration of notes on pages 21 and 22, we will already have realised that it is no use talking about the relative length of notes unless we have a regular space of a certain duration in which to place them. This restricted space is called the *bar*. The extent or limit of each bar is indicated by the *bar-lines* – these are the vertical lines running across the stave which we see on the sheet of music. The bar has two main purposes. (1) It chops the music up into equal lengths so that we can see how our various notes balance one another and make melodies. (2) It imposes a rhythmic pattern on the music – this we will examine in a moment.

Time signature.   Bar lines.

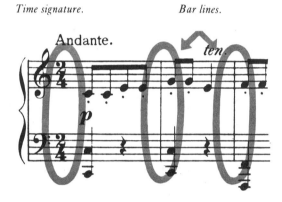

CHRISTOPH WILLIBALD VON GLUCK (1714-1787) *Germany*
After the pioneer work of composers like Monteverdi and Purcell, opera went through a period when it became increasingly slight and artificial. Gluck did much to restore it to its earlier glory. At the same time he took opera an important step forward. He made the characters in his operas act like real people, rather than puppets, and showed how dramatic and full of emotion an opera could be. With these reforms Gluck paved the way, first for Mozart, and later for Wagner and Verdi, who were to write the grandest of all operas. Gluck's opera *Orfeo ed Euridice*, based on the story of Orpheus in the Underworld from Greek mythology, is one of the earliest operas still to be regularly performed.

An artist's representation of simple and complex rhythms.

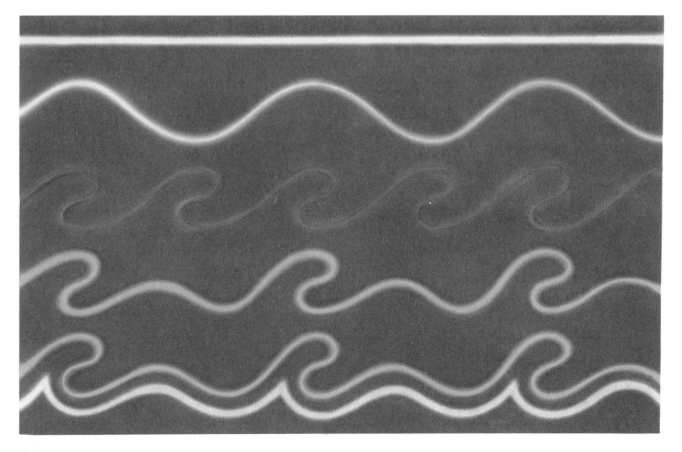

23

Let us look at our piano score again on page 20. At the beginning of the piece after the treble and bass clef signs there is written what looks like a fraction. This is the *time-signature*. It tells us how many beats there are to each bar, and what sort of beats they are. In our Haydn score the time-signature is $\frac{2}{4}$ (two-four), which means that there are two quarter-notes to a bar, or two crotchets to the bar.

So in one bar of this particular piece of music we can get either one minim, or two crotchets, or four quavers, or 8 semi-quavers, and so on. Or a mixture of these notes. The bar must always be completely filled either by notes to the correct value or a mixture of notes and rests.

Take the first eight bars. They contain (1) 4 quavers (2) 2 quavers and 1 crotchet (3) 4 quavers (4) 2 quavers and 1 crotchet (5) 4 quavers (6) 2 quavers and 1 crotchet (7) 4 quavers (8) 1 crotchet, 1 quaver and 1 quaver rest. A fairly simple sum to work out in this case. The total in each bar always adds up to 2 quarter-notes, or 2 crotchets.

If the music had been marked $\frac{4}{4}$ there would have been 4 crotchets in each bar. This is also known as common time and is sometimes indicated by 𝄴

If it had been marked $\frac{3}{4}$ there would have been three crotchets in each bar. This is three-four or waltz time.

There are many variants. It might by $\frac{2}{2}$ which would indicate two minims to each bar, that is two half-notes; it might be $\frac{6}{8}$ which means six eighth-notes or six quavers. It is also possible to have time-signatures such as $\frac{5}{4}$ or $\frac{9}{8}$.

Returning to Haydn once more, you can now measure out this $\frac{2}{4}$ rhythm of the slow movement of the 'Surprise' symphony by banging out 2 beats to the bar and seeing where the notes come in relation to the beat. Some come on it, and some between it, on what is called the *off-beat* part of the bar.

If the time-signature had been $\frac{3}{8}$ Haydn might have written his melody like this:

or like this in $\frac{3}{4}$ time:

or he could have had it in $\frac{6}{8}$ time like this:

Each way it is recognisably the same melody but has a different character. However, Haydn wanted it in $\frac{2}{4}$ time, and we will abide by his decision and keep it that way. It certainly sounds best like that.

By emphasising the first beat of each bar we may begin to feel how the music is splitting itself up into balanced sections and are ready to have a look at the structure of a melody.

Melody

Melody is the least scientific part of music. In fact, you might say that there is no science about it at all. Anybody might write a good melody – whether he could make it into a composition and harmonise it properly is another matter.

Melody is what stays in our minds – the string of notes that errand-boys traditionally whistle. Whether the next note goes up or down, or how long or how short the individual notes are, is purely a matter of inspiration and taste. The test of a good melody is its appeal to listeners – each one of whom likes a different kind of melody anyway.

The slow movement of the 'Surprise' is just about as simple and basic a melody as you can get, so let us have a look at it. Although the actual contours of a melody are not governed by any rules, there are certain ways in which it must behave if it is going to be recognisable as a melody. First of all, it will divide itself up into definite sections, comprising a certain number of bars, and these sections will give it an overall sense of balance and form.

This particular melody is 32 bars in length. It splits itself into four well-balanced sections of 8 bars (nearly all melodies are in 8 or multiples of 8 bars) and these are again split into phrases of 2 bars – also balancing. Here is the old mathematical science creeping in again, satisfying our sense of balance, our desire for symmetry which is so much a part of both traditional and classical art forms.

Just as in talking, our voice follows certain *cadences* (that is another word for inflections, movements up and down in pitch which clearly indicate whether we are merely pausing for breath, finishing a statement, asking a question or exclaiming in surprise), so does a melody use similar cadences. Cadences cannot be fully explained until we understand more about harmony, but it will be possible to get the feel of them by following Haydn's melody through, step by step. As we follow the melody we must beat time. It will be easiest if we give four beats to each bar – in this case, two strong beats with two slightly weaker beats in between, or, as the piece of music is in $\frac{2}{4}$ time we could count each bar out as one-and two-and / one-and two-and. Once we are certain how we are splitting up the bars we could try counting 1-da-da-da / 2-da-da-da / 3-da-da-da – and so on, so that we can tell how many bars have been played.

So Haydn starts with his simple melodic phrase covering two bars, thus. You can feel that very slight pause at the end and how this phrase asks to be answered by another.

Now he gives his answer. Notice how perfectly this phrase balances the last one, not only in length, completing four bars and again ending on a note which asks for the melody to continue, but also by coming down in pitch more or less by the same amount that the first phrase went up:

Now we have four bars of music nicely balanced. These seem to ask for another four bars to make the balance right once more. So Haydn repeats his first phrase:

but balances it this time with something quite different which takes us up in the air a bit more. The note that ends the eight bars has a little more finality about it, but it is still not an ending note. This we know must be C, because that is the *key* we are in.

FRANZ JOSEF HAYDN (1732-1809) *Austria*
This book is written around the work of Haydn because the 104 symphonies that he wrote were so vital in making the symphony the form in which the great European composers like Beethoven, Schubert and Brahms wrote their most important works. Haydn was a very pleasant and easy-going man with none of the fiery, poetical temperament of the typical 'romantic' writer, and his music is very like his character. Although it has a few stormy moments it is mainly calm, balanced, grave but with many touches of humour. Haydn's symphonies were written in a shapely, well-planned form that later composers used as a model for their own. The most popular have nicknames like the 'Surprise', the 'Clock' and the 'Military'. He also wrote in a similar way in his chamber and piano music and was most impressive in his wonderful choral works, e.g. *The Creation* and *The Seasons*.

So having written eight bars, but still not having come to a conclusive ending (by the melody coming to rest on a note of finality), we know that there must be at least another eight bars to come in order to balance the first eight. You get the idea now – 2 bars balancing 2, 4 bars balancing 4, 8 bars balancing 8 – and so on. In fact, what Haydn does now is to repeat the first eight bars almost exactly – the only difference being the loud 'surprise' chord at the end which goes right up in the air this time instead of dropping down to the lower G. It does, however, still end on G and it still does not sound as if the melody has concluded.

So off we must go again. As we have completed 16 bars of music without coming to an end we must now have at least another 16 to round things off in a balanced way.

This time Haydn goes off on a new tack, a sort of interlude which changes the character of the melody for the first time, the two-bar phrase

answered by another two bars of the same kind with that D sharp at the end definitely leading us to something interesting:

which is, in fact, two bars that are rather like the first two bars

but climbing higher and ending on a definite questioning high E, rather like a raising of the eyebrows:

And now, a rather neat little two-bar phrase answers this question and actually ends up on the key note of C:

This could be the end of the melody, but something tells us that it is not complete. The first 16 bars have only been balanced so far by another 8. Another 8 bars are needed to round it off properly. Haydn decides there shall be no more new ventures at this stage and repeats these last 8 bars again exactly. (In the score he varies the sound by calling in more instruments to play them.)

Thus we have a simple 32-bar melody, yet one which is full of light-hearted little twists, surprises (intentional and otherwise) and a surprising amount of variety.

This A-A-B-A form is a very frequent one and the basis of many popular songs: the melody stated in 4, or 8 bars, repeated in the next 4 or 8, a 4 or 8-bar interlude generally referred to as the *bridge*, and then the original 4 or 8 bars repeated again with a final cadence at the end. Here is a good example of this kind of popular melody:

The Foggy, Foggy Dew Suffolk folk song

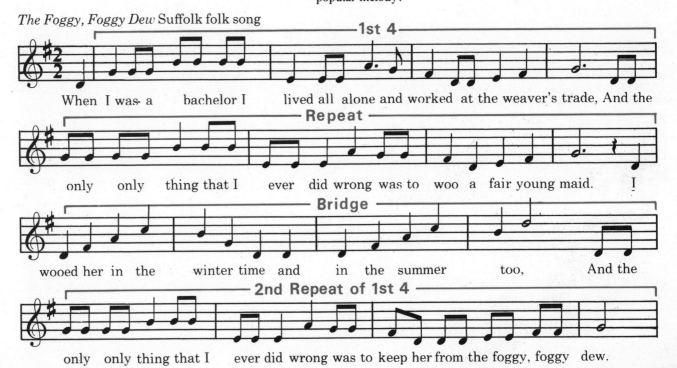

26

'The Concert' by Tournier. A 17th century group playing cello, spinet, violin and lute.

WOLFGANG AMADEUS MOZART (1756-1791) *Austria*

Mozart was the most amazing genius in musical history. He was recognised as an exceptional pianist when he was only six and was already composing excellent music when he was seven. Altogether he wrote over 700 works (with hardly a dull one among them) but he was so unworldly and often unlucky that he was reduced to poverty, died young and was buried in an unknown grave. He carried on the work of Haydn in the symphony and string quartet (also writing a group of superb string quintets) and developed the piano concerto. The operas *The Marriage of Figaro* (1786), *Don Giovanni* (1787) and *The Magic Flute* (1791) show us Mozart's equal mastery of the human voice and his wonderful sense of the theatre.

Part of Haydn's original score of the Slow Movement of the 'Surprise' Symphony.

Every musical composition contains a different melody. By coincidence, or even by intent some have very similar melodies, but this still leaves thousands of possible ways of arranging the basic 12 notes or tones of the *chromatic scale* (i.e. all the notes between C and C). Many ways have been found, and many more ways will be worked out by future composers. So it would be impossible to explore melody thoroughly or even cover all the different kinds. But here are a few well-known examples that indicate the enormous range of melodic style and mood that is possible in composing.

(a)

The formal classical melody from a sonatina by Clementi

(b)

The simple melancholy of the folk song *Londonderry Air* Irish folk song

(c)

A light-hearted rather frivolous melody *Humoreske* Op. 101. No. 7 by Dvořák

(d)

Lightly romantic Berceuse from the opera *Jocelyn* by Godard

(e)

In the grand style, Theme from Piano Concerto No. 1 Op. 23 by Tchaikovsky

(f)

The swirling glitter of the waltz from *Wiener Blut* by Johann Strauss

Scales and Keys

Now we come to the most involved part of the 'Science' – but, for this reason, probably the most interesting. Before we can talk about harmony, even basic harmony, it is useful to know how musical *keys* are decided. By harmony, we mean here the basic classical harmony that has been the material of European music of the last few centuries, the harmony of Mozart and Beethoven; what is academically called *diatonic* harmony – harmony confining itself to the basic scales. This does not apply to all music. Eastern music is based on an entirely different system, and modern European music has moved away from diatonic harmony as composers have become less content to stick to the textbook rules. We shall discuss some of the modern methods later.

We have already said that if we play the white notes of the piano from C to C we have played a *scale*. This scale has a ring of familiarity about it because it is the scale that is the basis of most of the music that we know. It is the scale that we follow out of habit when we use the *tonic sol-fa* method and sing:

doh, ray, me, fah, soh, lah, te, doh

Play these notes on the piano and the obvious thing that should strike you is the sense of finality when we come to that last C (or *doh*). If we end on the B (aptly called the leading note), there is a sense of incompleteness. When we move to the C you can feel that the scale has been finished off. We might describe C as the home-note, and if we think of our scale as a *melody* (which it is, even if a very unadventurous one) then the fact that it wants to end on C is further proof (if we need any) that our piece is in the key of C.

LUDWIG VAN BEETHOVEN (1770–1827) *Germany*
Still working on the models that Haydn and Mozart had created but finding ways of making music far more expressive and powerful, Beethoven wrote nine magnificent symphonies, five piano concertos, a violin concerto and other works for the orchestra. Best known of the symphonies are No. 3, the great 'Eroica'; No. 5, with its famous 'Victory' opening; No. 6, the lyrical 'Pastoral'; and No. 9, the monumental 'Choral', which adds voices to the orchestra. Beethoven wrote two other major vocal works, the opera *Fidelio*, and the *Missa Solemnis*. However, he reserved much of his finest thinking for his piano sonatas and string quartets. Many people consider the six quartets he wrote at the end of his life to be the greatest pieces of music ever composed.

An Indian dancer. Eastern music is based on an entirely different system to the one which is used in most music with which we are familiar.

29

Now if we played the scale G to G on the white notes of the piano we would have a slightly different sort of scale. It is a scale or *mode* (the old name for scale) which has gone out of fashion and does not sound quite right to our ears which are now so used to the major scale (or the *Ionian mode* as it was called). Without going into complicated reasons for it, we will simply accept the fact that European music gradually adopted the Ionian mode and, today referred to as the major mode or scale, it is the basis of most of our music.

Playing from G to G you will find, in fact, after a bit of experimentation that if you play F sharp instead of F each time then you have a correct major scale, sounding very like the C major except that it is higher up. The *root* note or basic note now happens to be G and it makes use of one of the black notes, but otherwise it sounds much the same.

Now we can do this by starting and finishing on any note of the piano. If we start on D we find that we have to play F sharp and C sharp before we have a correctly sounding major scale beginning and ending on D.

We have done this by ear – by listening to the sound. We can also do it on paper, working out the characteristics of each key by applying a formula.

Ravi Shankar playing the sitar, a stringed Indian instrument. The sitar, made of a gourd cut in half by the core, has seven main strings fastened to pegs on the neck and the sides, including the side strings used both for the drone and rhythmic accompaniment. 11 or 12 sympathetic strings running parallel to the main strings are tuned to the scale of the melody which is being played. The sitar is played with a wire plectrum and is so difficult that it takes many years to master the technique.

Taking the scale of C again (and remembering what we have already said about semitones and whole tones on pages 14 and 15), then the scale of C goes along like this: C to D – whole tone; D to E – whole tone; E to F – a semitone; F to G – a whole tone; G to A – a whole tone; A to B – a whole tone; B to C – semitone.

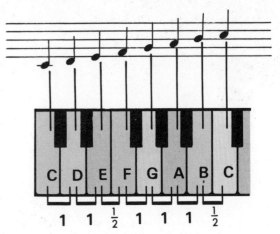

In other words the pattern of the major scale of C is: whole tone – whole tone – semitone – whole tone – whole tone – whole tone – semitone. And this is the pattern that any major scale follows. So if we start on D you can see that F sharp and C sharp must be played to keep to this pattern. What our ears are picking out is the jump from one note to the next and telling us if it is right or wrong.

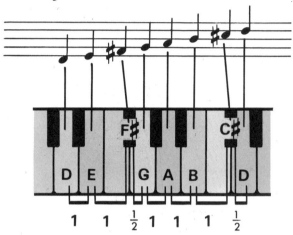

As it makes the page a little crowded if we have to keep putting the sharp and flat signs in (collectively known as *accidentals*), we simply put two sharp signs in the F and C positions at the beginning of the line, from which we now know that the piece of music is in D and that whenever we come to an F or a C we sharpen them.

If occasionally we want any extra sharps or flats we can still use the sharp or flat sign. These then are properly called accidentals, that is, notes sharpened or flattened that are not essential to or part of the key, or notes made natural or open when they would not normally be so.

The accidental sharpening or flattening of a note applies to the bar that it occurs in. If it is not so marked again in the next bar it is assumed to have returned to its normal pitch (a). If we want to make this understood we can use the *natural* sign ♮ which clearly indicates a return to the normal note. If we want it to return

GIOACCHINO ROSSINI (1792-1868) *Italy*
Following in the footsteps of earlier Italian opera composers who had tried to write music that simply showed off the beauties of the human voice (they called it *bel canto*), Rossini was mostly content to follow their example. But occasionally, as in his *Barber of Seville* – one of the most perfect comic operas of all time – he found the way to add warmth, life and humour to the traditional style. Most of his operas are only just being discovered again, having been forgotten, apart from their sparkling overtures which are played everywhere. Rossini was very famous in his day but became tired of the hectic life and retired to Paris where he simply wrote small pieces of music for his own amusement and one splendid, very operatic, choral work, the *Stabat Mater* (1832).

to normal before the end of the bar then we must always use the appropriate sign (b).

A piece of music in a major scale can be based on any of the white or black notes of the piano. It entirely depends on which note you begin and end your scale as to the number of sharps

31

C

F
One flat
Bb

Bb
2 flats
Bb & Eb

Eb
3 flats
Bb Eb & Ab

Ab
4 flats
Bb Eb Ab & Db

G
One sharp
F#

D
2 sharps
F# & C#

A
3 sharps
F# C# & G#

E
4 sharps
F# C# G# & D#

or flats that have to be included, in order to conform to the pattern of a major scale. Some commonly used keys are shown above.

Play all these scales and get used to the feel of the different keys. Although they are physically the same, each one has a slightly different nature. The flat keys sound mellower and grander, the sharp keys sound brighter and more colourful. Generally speaking, although it is harder to play in keys that have a lot of sharps and flats, they sound much more interesting than the simpler keys like C, G and F which have fewer accidentals (sharps and flats).

So far we have talked about the *major* scales and keys. The matter does not end here. There is another set of scales or keys in common use known as the *minor*. We shall not complicate matters here by examining the characteristics of minor scales (which are rather more involved than major scales). You can venture into this territory if and when you decide you would like to learn more about music outside the scope of this book.

Harmony

Harmony occupies the main part of a study of the theory of music, a big and involved subject, fascinating and rewarding beyond measure. All we can do here is to say what harmony is, and show it in its simplest form, based on our knowledge of the major keys.

Harmony is simply the sounding of two or more notes together so that they blend in a pleasing or interesting way. Simple harmony is the placing of other notes below or above the notes of our melody line. If these other notes themselves form a second melody, then we call it *counterpoint*. Naturally, in an orchestral score, where each of the instruments might be playing its own melody or theme, there is a great deal of counterpoint. At the same time, wherever the notes coincide and produce a *chord* we also have harmony. We look at melody and counterpoint horizontally; at harmony vertically.

The slow movement of the 'Surprise' symphony is in the basic key of C. C is the basic or *tonic* note of this key. Therefore the basic chords are all based on C. They are called the tonic chords. The simplest chord is C with the notes a third and a fifth degree above it. The third (remember that we count C as one) is E, the fifth is G. These notes fall neatly on the next two lines of the musical stave. Such a chord, because it contains two jumps of a third, C to E and E to G, is called a *triad*.

Try playing these three notes together – C, E and G – and hear how well they blend. Played as we have written them with C at the bottom, the chord is said to be in the *root* position. But you can now put those notes in any order (or add more of them – that is to say, more C's, E's or G's) and you still have what is fundamentally the same chord. Put another way round these chords are called 'inversions' of the root chord or triad:

FRANZ SCHUBERT (1797-1828) *Austria*
Although he wrote some fine symphonies, the best known being No. 8, the 'Unfinished', many operas which are now almost completely unknown, and a great deal of splendid chamber-music, including the delightful 'Trout' quintet, Schubert will chiefly be remembered as the greatest song writer of all time. He seemed to be able to write melodies as fast as he could put them on to paper. Then he always found just the right sort of piano part to help the singer to give the best effect. The perfect songs that resulted inspired many composers including Brahms, Schumann, Richard Strauss and Hugo Wolf (1860-1903). Many of the finest songs are included in two groups which have a story to tell; *Die Winterreise* (1827) – 'Winter Journey', and *Die schöne Mullerin* (1823) – 'The Fair Maid of the Mill'. Like Mozart, Schubert died tragically young.

Harmony and Discord. The colours in the horizontal and vertical lines of squares harmonise with each other, but the colours in the diagonal line certainly do not.

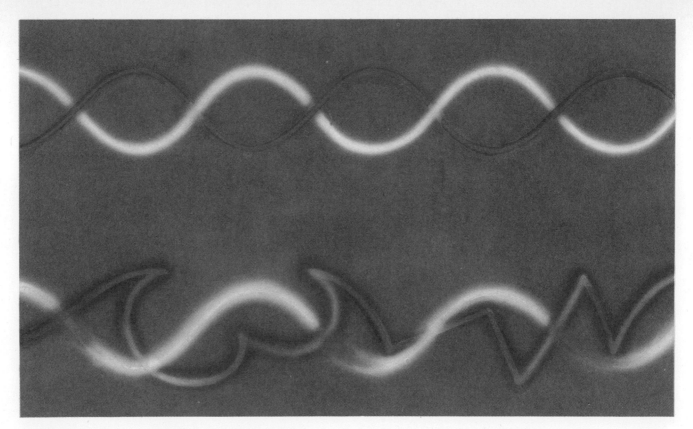

Harmony and Discord. An artist's impression of harmony and discord represented in colour.

Each note of the scale has a different name. The first note, as we know already, is called the tonic. The rest are named as follows:

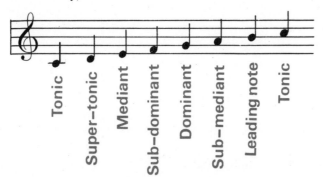

The other chords that are important in the key of C are those based on the dominant and sub-dominant which are, in this case, G and F. The triad on G is G,B,D, and very often it has the 7th added as well, which is F (in which case this chord is known as the

dominant 7th). The triad based on F is F,A,C – this is the chord of the sub-dominant. When we know these four basic chords,

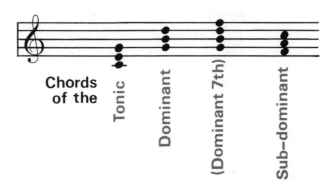

surprising as it may seem, we know the rudiments of harmony.

Such harmony is sufficient for writing simple and effective music; for example, most folk and traditional songs, popular songs and ballads. Even a great deal of orchestral music is effectively based on just these harmonies. The first six bars of the slow movement of our Haydn symphony confines itself to these three chords:

34

HECTOR BERLIOZ (1803-1869) *France*

Berlioz is remembered as a composer who helped to change the orchestra from the modest group that it was in the days of Haydn to the splendid sounding array of instruments that it is today. He wrote valuable books on the subject of writing for the orchestra and also on the art of conducting. The audiences of his day were startled (and sometimes annoyed) by the adventurous new sounds that he got with the large orchestra that he used. His most lasting work is the strangely beautiful *Symphonie fantastique* (1830-1) and several of his overtures are frequently played. His operas, which are generally too long for the ordinary opera-house, are occasionally heard.

'Coronation of the Virgin' by Fra Angelico. Angels are shown playing trumpets while the central figure plucks a lute. On the right a bowed lute is being played.

A recent popular modern folk group, 'The Seekers'.

Harmonic Complications

All rules, in art, exist to be broken. In a book like this we lay down some basic rules. The composer spends his time trying to expand them, as you will see if you study music more.

A musical composition could remain within the limits we have outlined above. But if a whole symphony stayed there it would get monotonous. The trend, in musical history, as in the history of any art, is for technical advancement. In other words, the composer naturally wishes to extend the boundaries of his art. Music and musical harmony have been extended in various stages, amongst which the following have been obvious steps.

1. *Modulation*. Instead of staying in the same key throughout a piece you change (or modulate) the music into other keys. In bars 7 and 8 of our score Haydn modulates into the key of G, firstly by introducing the dominant 7th chord of D7 which is the dominant of G and which naturally leads us into the key of G itself. This is only a temporary modulation as he immediately goes back into C in the 9th bar. The temporary modulation does, however, help his 'surprise' tactics, particularly when in the 16th bar he plays the chord of G as loud as he can after an extremely soft and gentle passage of music.

It is easy to modulate into a nearly related key.

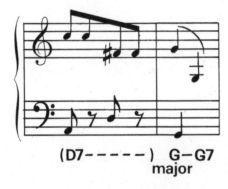

(D7 – – – – –) G – G7
major

By this we mean keys of a like character. The near relations of C are naturally F and G which have only one flat and one sharp respectively, and the minor keys of A, E and D which have similar characteristics.

Gradually composers became more daring in their modulations. Schubert, we find, was fond of sudden modulations. Not sudden by modern standards, but still not conforming to the polite requirements of the conservative academic world. He would happily jump from G to E flat and back again without any very elaborate preparation. In stricter harmony we are taught to modulate in careful steps, gradually introducing notes from the new key.

Sudden change from G to Eb from a Schubert waltz

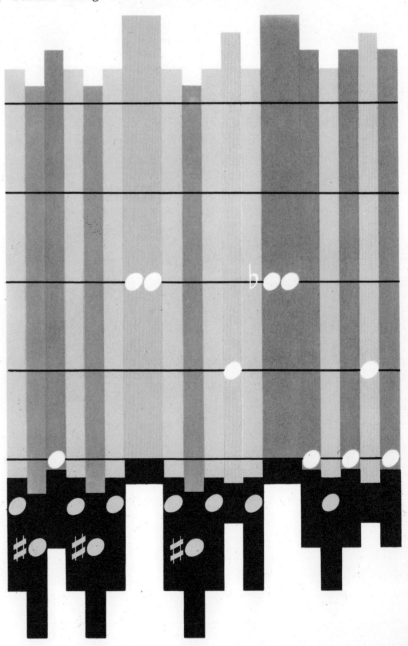

Diagram showing the change from G to E flat in a Schubert Waltz, the notes represented by colour changes (see keyboard in colour on p. 14).

Following this particular trend composers made more and more daring leaps into strange keys, often ending up in a different key than they started off in. Music which abides by the rules and keeps one key in mind throughout is called *tonal* – it revolves around the *tonic* key. Music which leaps about and refuses to have a fixed basic key is called *atonal*.

Atonal writing from a Piano Piece by Schönberg

2. *Chromatic Harmony*. Music which confines itself, apart from occasional accidentals to the notes of the scale is called diatonic. When it regularly uses notes not in the scale as part of its harmonies, it is making use of the notes of the chromatic scale, a scale from C to C, for example, which includes all the notes – black and white.

If we look at a piece of music by a 20th century composer, Maurice Ravel, we can see how advanced these harmonies had become by this period of musical history, particularly when we compare it with the elemental harmonies of the Haydn symphony.

from *L'Heure Espagnole* by Ravel

FELIX MENDELSSOHN (1809-1847) *Germany*
While still in his teens Mendelssohn wrote some of his most endearing music such as the magical overture, *A Midsummer Night's Dream*. Later he wrote a complete set of music for a German production of the play, including the well-known *Scherzo* and *Wedding March*. Apart from these he is best known for his lively 4th Symphony, the 'Italian', the *Hebrides* overture (also known as *Fingal's Cave*) and for his great oratorio *Elijah*, tremendously popular in Victorian England. Written for the piano, his famous *Songs Without Words* were short descriptive pieces played in every drawing-room.

Ravel's opera 'L'Heure Espagnole' is one of this composer's most colourful works.

Twelve-Tone Music

This modern way of getting rid of the shackles of diatonic harmony was developed in the 20th century by composers like Arnold Schönberg (1874-1951) and his disciples, Anton Webern (1883-1945) and Alban Berg (1885-1935).

The basic idea was to forget all about keys and to write music based on all the twelve notes or tones of the chromatic scale. It is obvious that these twelve notes can be arranged in many hundreds of ways. The system that Schönberg invented said that you started with your *tone-row* or series, that is a certain arrangement of the twelve notes (only using each one once), and then you always kept them in this order throughout the composition. Here is an example:

But having established your pattern, you could then do a number of things with it, like reversing it or turning it upside-down. Such music is itself bound by as many restrictions as the old diatonic music – possibly the reason why it has not superseded the older methods. At first twelve-note music sounded outlandish, rather weird and dry. But as more composers have used it skilfully and more naturally (and made the rules less rigid) we have become used to it; we gradually become used to everything that starts out by being revolutionary. It is now possible to listen to twelve-note music without it bothering us a great deal.

Schönberg was one of the inventors of 'twelve note' music and his opera 'Moses and Aaron' is written in this idiom.

Jazz

At the turn of the century a new kind of music called *jazz* arrived on the scene. It grew out of the folk music of the negro slaves who worked on the cotton plantations in the southern states of the USA. The first jazz bands performed in the city of New Orleans, which had a large negro population. Then as negro people travelled north to cities like St. Louis and Chicago in search of work, so jazz spread first to other parts of the USA and finally to Europe.

What is jazz? Melodically, there is no firm boundary that tells us that one melody is a jazz melody and one is not. So there is really nothing new from the melodic angle except a few obvious tricks such as the deliberate use of flattened notes where the normal note might have been expected, such as in George Gershwin's '*Somebody loves me*'.

In fact, these characteristics belong to what is known as 'traditional jazz', that is, jazz played in its original style. A lot of popular music is still based on this particular idiom, but jazz itself has gone on developing, and much modern jazz is as difficult to understand as the music of other modern composers.

ROBERT SCHUMANN (1810-1856) *Germany*
Robert Schumann was everyone's idea of the 'romantic' composer; his life was tragically short and full of sorrow. After being a brilliant pianist he injured his hand and had to give up playing. His personal life was full of difficulties and he managed his artistic career very badly. After suffering a nervous breakdown he tried to commit suicide but was saved – only to die two years later in a mental home. His best music was in his shorter works. As a song-writer he almost rivalled Schubert and in his numerous piano pieces he was a vivid painter of scenes and portraits. His sets of piano music including the delightful *Carnaval* and the *Kinderscenen* (Scenes of Childhood) are his most lasting works.

Duke Ellington is one of the most famous of modern jazz musicians and composers.

There is nothing particularly new about jazz harmonies. In fact, jazz uses the standard musical harmony and even the most modern jazz usually borrows from what academic composers have attempted before. The slightly 'different' harmonic flavour of jazz is a result of jazz being *improvised* music. Much of it is made up at the moment of playing it. Because two or three instruments are moving about fairly freely, although with a constant attention to the harmonic structure of the piece of music they are playing, they are bound to indulge in a few clashes and unusual modulations, especially as they often flatten or sharpen notes to a degree that cannot be shown by the normal notation. If an instrument is playing *legato*, that is sliding from one note to the next without a pause (the trombone for example can do this very easily), it is bound to be using not only the tones and semitones of the scale but also the degrees that lie between these. The accidental or intentional use of these areas of sound gives jazz its rather odd flavour. But these are only momentary diversions from tonality; the players are not deliberately indulging in the use of quarter-tones, a system that has been explored in an academic way without much success. There have been pianos constructed capable of playing a quarter-tone scale. In Western music, where diatonic music has held sway for so long, we are not yet ready to investigate these possibilities, although our ears can quickly get used to Eastern music where quarter-tones and other divisions of the scale have been in use for centuries.

We have no accepted way of writing harmonies which are not strictly within the diatonic scale (although a way of writing quarter-tones has been devised) and we are even more restricted when we try to give notes time values that are different from the normal divisions which we have already explained (pages 21-22). Where jazz differs mostly from other music is in its rhythms – not so much the basic underlying rhythm which is usually un-varied and metronomic, but in its melodic rhythms. It has been written many times that the basic element of jazz is the continued and varied use of *syncopation*. Syncopation is the playing and stressing of melodic notes away from the main beats of the bar; playing them where they would not normally be expected. One

One of the foremost traditional jazz musicians in Britain, Acker Bilk created a distinctive sound as a clarinettist.

can create syncopation by using dotted notes but this is not very subtle. It is the sort of syncopation that you will find in *ragtime* (an early kind of jazz, mainly music written especially for the piano and based on the cakewalk and other jerky French-Negro dances) and the sort of syncopation that composers like Debussy and Stravinsky have exploited in their parodies of jazz:

Passage from *Maple Leaf Rag* by Scott Joplin

FREDERIC CHOPIN (1810-1849) *Poland*
Chopin has been called the 'poet of the piano', as most of his music was written for that instrument. And the particular eloquence and expressiveness of his style makes his music some of the most distinctive ever written. Some of his ideas came from the national music of Poland and he wrote many mazurkas and polonaises in this style. He created a waltz that was ideal for the piano, and many nocturnes that showed how expressive the piano could be. His brilliant playing abilities were shown in the studies that he wrote, and in two fine sonatas. As a pianist he toured all over Europe but gradually he became a sick man and died at an early age.

But the true improvised jazz phrasing such as you get in the *blues* – a basic form of jazz in which it became noticeably different from the march character of ragtime, with the melody generally extending over groups of twelve bars rather than eight and with a melodic line that followed the natural inflections of the negro voice – used a kind of syncopation that was much subtler. Jazz rhythm could be analysed as being triple time imposed on duple time, even in the comparatively simple matter of writing three notes in place of two. We have seen how you do this on page 22 with the tied triplet. But if, for example, we only wanted to play the second note of that triplet in the place where it would normally fall there is no satisfactory way of writing it in isolation. If we wanted to impose six notes on two and then to write one of them alone, there is just no way to do it.

So we find that jazz phrasing is, at the moment, entirely up to the performer and the composer can only give an approximate idea of what he wants in the jazz idiom. Jazz is a performer's art. A jazz composer, like Duke Ellington, has to be a jazz musician as well, if he is to get a proper interpretation of his ideas. The only way to play jazz is by instinct and this is the great obstacle which prevents a symphony orchestra (probably made up of a greater percentage of non-jazz-minded musicians) being able to play true jazz. As younger and more sympathetic players and composers gradually absorb jazz into their thinking and playing, this problem may well be overcome.

Required notes ◯

Musical Language

We have touched briefly upon all the ingredients of music that are to be found in the pages of our chosen score – melody, harmony and rhythm – the three elements of music. We have seen how these are indicated by written music and how they can be translated into sound.

But if we played music as mathematically as it is written, it would soon become rather tedious. If we are going to interpret music in an interesting way we must make it expressive. This is the role of the musician.

The composer will try to indicate the speed, or tempo, of the music and variations of tempo; he will indicate the volume of sound he requires; he will suggest ways of phrasing, ways of playing notes and groups of notes that will help the player to get near to his original idea.

In the slow movement of the 'Surprise' symphony the first written instruction is *andante* which means that Haydn wants the music played smoothly and not too fast. This is a very vague sort of guidance and the actual speed will be varied a great deal by different conductors. Haydn marks the first eight bars *p* – meaning *piano*, the Italian for quietly. Later he asks for *pp* – double *piano* – even quieter; then suddenly demands an *ff* – double *forte* – very loud, for the 'surprise' chord. A very obvious marking, but the music would be pointless if it were not observed.

The dots underneath the notes mean that they are to be played sharply and detached – *staccato*, well separated rather than running into one another. The instruction *ten.* is an abbreviation of *tenuto* meaning that the composer would like you to hold those notes so marked a little longer than you normally would. *Pizz.* is an abbreviation of *pizzicato*, telling the musician to pluck the strings; while *arco* tells him to use the bow again.

These, and other musical terms that you are almost certain to meet with, are explained in the next few pages.

Terms Used in Music

Because so much of music's early history took place in Italy, Italian has become the universal language of music. Most of the commonly used musical terms, for example *allegro* and *andante*, are Italian and are used in all countries. Later in musical history, when other nations became more aware of their own musical heritage, composers started to use their native language so that we now have terms in German, French and English as part of our universal musical vocabulary. There are a great many words in this vocabulary – even a short dictionary would have to find room for about 500. The following list includes a few of the really essential descriptive words that you would find in most scores and are Italian unless otherwise stated.

Terms Concerning Speed or Tempo

The word tempo is often wrongly used as if it meant rhythm or time – people often talk of waltz tempo. Tempo means the speed or pace of the music. Just as the speed of a car is spoken of in miles per hour, so the speed of music is spoken of in terms of so many notes (generally quavers) per minute. An instrument which is used to measure these speeds is called a *metronome* which can be regulated to give so many ticks per minute and which can help you to play at fixed speeds. Some composers give exact metronome markings so that there can be no doubt as to the speed at which they want their music played, but most conductors have their own ideas as to what is *allegro* or *andante*, also varying it according to the piece being played, so there is little point in laying down an exact figure which each of these terms demands. They should be taken as an approximate indication of speed.

A metronome, a mechanical device, which can be set to beat out a regular rhythm at varying speeds.

Terms indicating a very slow tempo

ADAGIO – very slowly; at a leisurely pace.
GRAVE – slowly and solemnly.
LARGO – slowly and in a stately manner.
LENTO – very slowly.

Each of these terms means much the same in regard to pace but each suggests a different approach.

Terms indicating a moderate tempo

ANDANTE – smoothly, not too fast, not too slow.
ANDANTINO – at a gentle speed; a little faster than *andante*.
MODERATO – at a moderate speed.

Terms indicating a faster tempo

ALLEGRETTO – fairly brightly and in a lively manner; faster than *moderato*, not quite so fast as *allegro*.
ALLEGRO – at a lively pace, brightly.
VIVACE – full of life, probably rather faster than *allegro*.
PRESTO – quickly, at a dashing pace.
PRESTISSIMO – very quickly.

The above terms are also used as the names of movements or parts of a composition, or of whole compositions, that are to be played at the speed they suggest. So we talk of the *Allegro* movement of a symphony, or the *Andante*.

FRANZ LISZT (1811-1886) *Hungary*

Liszt will always be thought of as a pianist and as a writer for the piano although he wrote many great orchestral and vocal works. For he was, above all, a great 'virtuoso', a player who astounded everyone who heard him, and he wrote difficult and dazzling piano music to match his abilities as a player. He was also a fine organist. Some of his early music was simply an exciting display but later, when he became very religious and known as the Abbé Liszt, his music became much more serious. Many of his piano works are full of the folk tunes of his country and he is best-known for the exciting *Hungarian Rhapsodies*. A favourite occupation of his was to take the music of other composers and arrange it in complicated style for the piano.

Terms indicating an adjustment of tempo

ACCELERANDO – gradually becoming faster.
ALLARGANDO (ALLARG.) – becoming slower and broader, generally louder as well.
RITARDANDO (generally abbreviated to RITARD. or, RIT.) – a temporary and gradual slowing down, lingering. Often used to reduce the pace at the end of a piece.
STRINGENDO – a temporary quickening of pace.
A TEMPO – back to the original speed after some such change of pace.
TENUTO (usually written as TEN.) – holding or lingering upon a single note.

If a definite but brief pause is wanted after a note a FERMATA or pause sign is written over it thus: ⌒

43

Terms Concerning Expression

To give an even more explicit idea of the composer's intentions, these terms are used in addition to the indications of speed, and can either be added to the other terms as in *andante cantabile*, or be used alone sometimes setting the style of a whole section or sometimes just calling for a temporary effect.

AGITATO – in an agitated manner, disturbed.
BRAVURA – with great dash and energy.
CANTABILE – with great expression, as if the instrument were singing words.
ESPRESSIVO – a very general instruction to play expressively.
FURIOSO – furiously.

GRANDIOSO – in a grand, pompous manner.
GRAZIOSO – gracefully.
LEGATO – flowing smoothly, the notes melting into one another.
LEGGIERO – lightly.
PORTAMENTO – similar to LEGATO; gliding from one note to the next with as little break as possible; the opposite of STACCATO.
SCHERZANDO – in a light-hearted, jovial manner – hence a movement or composition called a SCHERZO.
SPIRITO – with spirit; full of zest.
STACCATO – the notes played crisply, as detached from one another as possible. Also indicated by dots written over or under the notes.
VIF (French) – in a lively manner.

FURIOSO

LEGATO

STACCATO

GRANDIOSO

SCHERZANDO

Terms Concerning Volume

PIANO – meaning quiet, written as *p*; with various degrees: *mezzo-piano*, fairly quiet, *mp*; and *pianissimo* – very quietly, written *pp* or with additional *p*'s emphasising the need to play as quietly as possible, *pppp*, etc.

Another Italian term is *sotto voce*, which also means very softly. The opposite extreme is:

FORTE – meaning loud, written as *f*; *mezzo-forte* – fairly loud, *mf*; and *fortissimo*, very loud, *ff*, or as many *f*'s as is felt necessary to emphasise the need for volume.

Forte-piano indicates the need for a momentary increase in volume, immediately returning to *piano*.

Adjustment of volume

CRESCENDO (*cresc.*) – growing gradually louder.
DECRESCENDO (*decresc.*) – growing gradually quieter.
Similarly, and perhaps more frequently used – DIMINUENDO (*dimin.* or *dim.*). Also *smorzando* (*smorz.*) – dying away to nothing.

FORZANDO – with sudden stress or emphasis – written *fz*. Also *sforzando*, *sf* or *sfz*.

A temporary stress or emphasis on a single note, *marcato*, is indicated thus —, a heavy line written over a note.

A series of cartoons by Hoffnung representing different musical terms.

GIUSEPPE VERDI (1813-1901) *Italy*
Verdi was the greatest of all the many great composers of opera who came from Italy. Compared to Wagner, in Germany, he wrote in an old-fashioned way but he was a fine master of his craft. After one or two unsuccessful early works he suddenly became very well-known when he wrote an opera called *Nabucco*. This contained a chorus of Hebrew slaves which so appealed to the Italians, at that time fighting for their political freedom, that it almost became a national anthem. His first great opera was *Rigoletto* (1851), quickly followed by *Il Trovatore* and *La Traviata* in 1853. One of his most spectacular works was *Aida* (1871) originally written for the opening of the Suez Canal. Finally, he turned to more dramatic and less conventional works which portrayed *Otello* (1887) and *Falstaff* (1893). Altogether he wrote over 30 operas, most of them very successful.

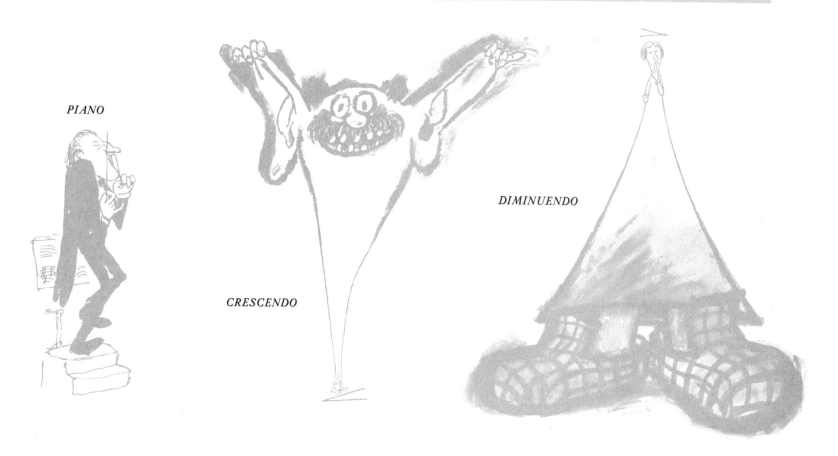

PIANO

CRESCENDO

DIMINUENDO

Part 3

The Instruments of the Orchestra

Now we have looked at the musical devices used in our score and understood their significance, the next point of interest is the musical instruments which the composer has at his disposal. Compared to the modern symphony orchestra, Haydn's requirements were very modest. The orchestra of his day was much smaller and used fewer kinds of instruments. But it had achieved, partly under his guidance, the balanced proportions which still seem right and logical today.

Some of the instruments that Haydn had at his disposal were much cruder than they are now, and the musicians were probably nowhere near as skilled as the modern orchestral musician. The brass instruments, for instance, were only just leaving the stage of their development at which they could only play the simple harmonic notes of the triad of the key to which they were tuned, like a bugle.

The orchestra is made up of four groups of instruments: the strings, the woodwind, the brass and the percussion. Because of their pleasantly mellow tones which can be heard for long periods without becoming monotonous or over-bearing, the strings are given the larger part in most scores and generally play for most of the time in any orchestral composition.

Part of the string section, the double-basses.

The leader of the orchestra is seated on the left-hand side by the conductor, the first violins ranged behind him.

Part of the woodwind section. In the foreground, a piccolo, and next, two flutes.

46

Because of the softness of tone there have to be more stringed instruments in the orchestra to balance the more penetrating tones of the wind instruments, which are used to add orchestral colour and are most effectively used in moderation. As orchestras became larger and composers more skilled in using the various possible effects, music became more colourful, more complex, more ambitious. The orchestra which Haydn used might be considered the basic orchestral unit.

It will be seen that his strings are continuously in operation. They consist of the *violins* split into two groups called *first* and *second violins* each playing a different part usually in close harmony; the *violas*, slightly larger instruments which play a similar part to the violins on lower harmonic notes; and the *cellos* and *double-basses* sharing a bass part which provides a rhythmical foundation. One of the first advances in orchestral writing after this period was the promotion of the cello to a more important and independent role.

In his woodwind section Haydn has 2 *flutes* (*flauti*); 2 *oboes* (*oboi*); 2 *bassoons* (*fagotti*). A surprising absentee is the *clarinet* which is now the leading member and the most fluent of the woodwind family. Another missing member is the *piccolo* which is a small higher-pitched flute.

RICHARD WAGNER (1813-1883) *Germany*

Wagner wrote operas which were as 'grand' as any operas are ever likely to be. Unlike Verdi, who was born in the same year, he soon started to experiment. He made the music mean just as much as the words, each character, each thought and mood represented by a musical theme. Everything about his work is big and powerful – huge orchestras, fantastic stage settings and great dramatic parts for the singers. Wagner based most of his operas on German folk legend and Teutonic mythology. His best-known operas, or 'music dramas' as he called them, are *Tannhäuser*, *Lohengrin*, *Tristan und Isolde*, *Die Meistersinger von Nürnberg*, and the four separate operas known collectively as *Der Ring des Nibelungen*.

Part of the brass section. In the foreground, three trumpets.

James Blades, who has combined a musical career as a tympanist and lecturer on percussion, is shown here playing the kettledrums. Behind him is a tam-tam.

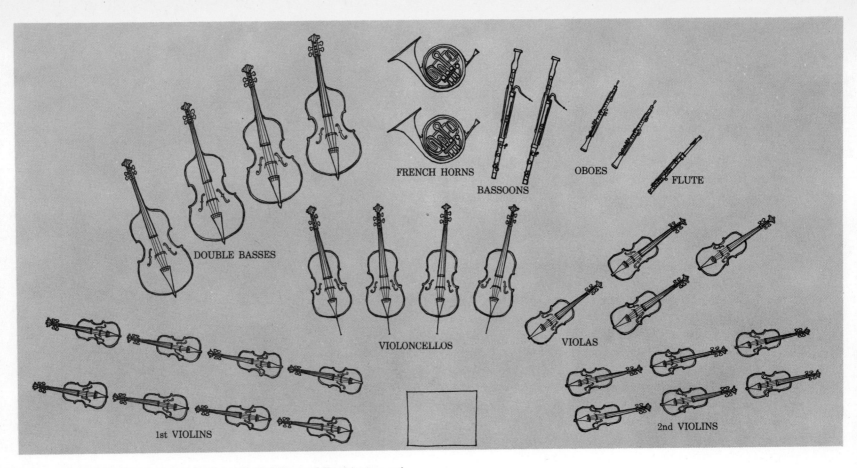

FRENCH HORNS   BASSOONS   OBOES   FLUTE

DOUBLE BASSES   VIOLONCELLOS   VIOLAS

1st VIOLINS   2nd VIOLINS

These two diagrams show (above) a typical orchestra of Haydn's time, and (below) a modern symphony orchestra. The conductor always stands at the front.

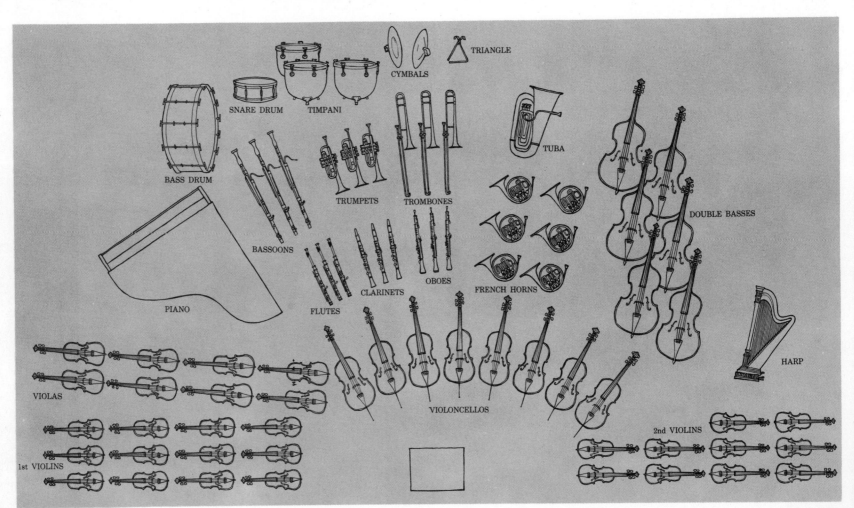

TRIANGLE   CYMBALS   TIMPANI   SNARE DRUM

BASS DRUM   TRUMPETS   TROMBONES   TUBA

BASSOONS   DOUBLE BASSES

PIANO   FLUTES   CLARINETS   OBOES   FRENCH HORNS   HARP

VIOLAS   VIOLONCELLOS   2nd VIOLINS

1st VIOLINS

The brass section is simply made up of two *horns* (*corni*) and two *trumpets* (*trombe*). In a modern orchestra one would certainly expect to find *trombones* and possibly a *tuba*.

The only percussion in Haydn's orchestra are two *timpani*, tunable drums tuned in the Andante to C and G. In other symphonies, he employs more percussion instruments than this, and the modern percussion section is often vast and varied, although the tuned timpani have always seemed an indispensable item.

Orchestration is a large subject and the composer should know something of the technique of playing and the limitations of each instrument even if he cannot possibly play them all.

A great 'orchestral' composer will think all the time of the combined sound. In other words, he does not write out his music as a piano piece and then dress it up for orchestra; but hears it right away as an orchestral sound, one big instrument with many working parts capable of infinitely varied effects.

The orchestra is not, of course, the only medium for making great music. Equally fine music is written for smaller chamber-groups (two or more instruments) and for solo performers. There is no doubt, however, that the rich, full and colourful sound of the orchestra is, to most people, the most exciting effect that music has to offer.

JACQUES OFFENBACH (1819-1880) *France*
While Wagner wrote serious opera, Offenbach with his genius for witty and sparkling music established the lightest kind of opera in his own little theatre in Paris. He called it *opéra bouffe*, musical entertainment variously called light opera, operetta, musical comedy, and today, the 'musical'. Inspired by Italian composers like Donizetti, in turn he influenced such writers as Johann Strauss and Sullivan. His *Orpheus in the Underworld* (1858), *La Belle Hélène* (1864) and *La Vie Parisienne* (1868) are all noted for their tunefulness and gaiety, though in his own lifetime Offenbach was sometimes in trouble on account of their biting wit and political satire. Finally, he wrote a great opera *The Tales of Hoffman* (1881).

This picture was taken on the famous last night of the London 'Proms'. The late Sir Malcolm Sargent is with the BBC Symphony Orchestra.

49

Stringed Instruments –
The Violin Family

All stringed instruments work on the principle of a note being produced by making a length of gut or wire vibrate and the sound being amplified by the hollow body of the instrument. The string is made to vibrate either by being plucked with the fingers or some small piece of material held in the fingers or by drawing a *bow* across it.

The bow is made of strands of horse-hair (nowadays nylon or some other synthetic material is often used) which are stretched fairly tightly across a shaped piece of wood – rather like the bow used to shoot arrows with, but with about 150 strands of the fine hairs and of a rather more elegant and elaborate shape. The bow hairs are rubbed with resin – a substance like hard glue which is found in wood – and this makes them grip the strings as the bow is moved across them. You can imagine how the bow pulls the string to one side and how the string, because of its own tension, slips back, and is then caught up again. This action, repeated many times, sets up one long smooth vibration, and consequently a note that will continue as long as the bow is moving.

One of the world's leading violinists, Yehudi Menuhin. This photograph clearly shows how the violin is held and played.

The violin. The player draws the bow over the strings.

Three conditions affect the pitch of the note that any string will produce. Its thickness, its length and its tension. The thicker the strings are the more slowly they vibrate and the deeper the note. A stringed instrument usually has at least four strings of graded thicknesses so that it can produce a wide range of notes, the thicker strings giving the deeper notes, the thinner ones the higher notes.

The length of the string is fixed by the length of the instrument. It can obviously only be varied by shortening it. This is done by pressing the string down with the fingers of the hand in the correct position on the *fingerboard* of the instrument.

All the instruments of the violin family are of similar shape and are made up of similar parts. It is their size which distinguishes them. The violin is the smallest and therefore has the highest range of notes; the viola is slightly bigger. Both of these are held under the chin and are light enough to be supported in this way. Although the left hand helps to hold the instrument, it is mainly occupied by the task of finding the correct position for each note on the strings, while the right hand holds the bow. The cello is much bigger and is stood on the floor, the player holding it between his knees and, of necessity, always in a sitting position. The double-bass is larger still and of such a height that the player must either stand up or use a high stool.

ANTON BRUCKNER (1824-1896) *Austria*

Following in the steps of Haydn, Mozart and Beethoven came a number of great 'romantic' composers in Germany and Austria who wrote 'symphonic' music on a grand scale. Like Beethoven, Bruckner wrote nine symphonies that are big, noble works full of rich music. Although his works seem large and complicated, Bruckner was at heart a simple and religious man. He allowed all kinds of people, including his pupils, to re-write and arrange his music for him and the musical scholars are only just sorting out what Bruckner himself really wrote, so that we can hear his works as he originally intended them.

*Note the comparative size of the string instruments (*Left to right, *violin, violin, double bass, viola and cello*).*

51

Each of these instruments has a different set of strings – the double-basses thicker and longer and therefore deeper in tone, the violins the shortest and highest in tone. Their *open* notes, that is, the strings played just as they are without being shortened by the fingers, are as follows:

Violins: G D A E
Violas: C G D A
Cellos: C G D A (Octave lower)
D. Bass: Generally E A D G

The player cannot make the string sound lower than its open note because he cannot lengthen it. If he starts on his thickest and lowest string, therefore, its open note is the lowest note that he can play. On the cello, for example, this would be C. By placing his fingers on the string in the correct position and pushing the string against the fingerboard

he can produce these notes on his C string:
D E F
or, by adapting the position of his fingers, slightly, the inter-

mediate notes between these, that is C sharp or D flat, D sharp or E flat and F sharp.

So, on the C string he plays the chromatic scale C, C sharp, D, D sharp, E, F, F sharp. As his next string is G he now moves to that and moves upwards through the scales placing his fingers in the correct positions to obtain the notes G sharp or A flat, A, A sharp or B flat, B, C, C sharp or D flat.

Now he can move to the D string and continue upwards by finding D sharp or E flat, E, F, F sharp or G flat, G, G sharp or A flat.

He continues up the scale by moving to his highest string. By continuing to move up this string until he reaches the end of the fingerboard he will be able to produce a note which will be round about A, two octaves above the open note.

While he shortens the strings in this manner with his left hand (this is called *stopping* the strings), he is drawing his bow across the same string (or plucking the string with a finger) to produce the required note.

He can play and finger two strings at once to produce a simple harmony – this is called *double-stopping*, or even three strings at once, *triple-stopping* – making sure that his bow is touching the required number of strings instead of just one.

But before he plays his instrument at all, the musician must make sure that it is *in tune*, that is to say that all the strings are playing the correct open note in relation to the other instruments. For the pitch of the string depends not only on its thickness and length but also on its tautness. The tighter it is the higher the note. So the player can tune his instrument by tightening or slackening the strings by turning the pegs at the top of the neck around which the strings are wound.

If he is a soloist playing a sonata to piano accompaniment he will tune his instrument against the notes of the piano. In the orchestra the oboist generally sounds an A and everyone tunes from this. All the violin family have an open A string. To make sure that the standard pitch is being used it is possible to obtain

Cello. First position of the fingers.

Second position.

Third position.

tuning forks, shaped pieces of metal which give out an accurately pitched note when struck.

The VIOLIN and the other instruments of the violin family are a development of the *viols*, six-stringed instruments of various sizes played with a bow. The violin as we know it was mainly developed in Italy in the 16th century. Several famous families of violin-makers perfected violins that are named after them – the Stradivarius or the Guarnerius, for example

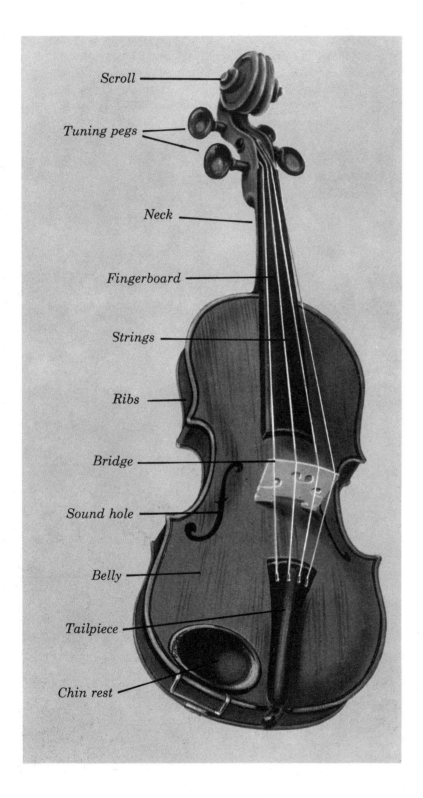

Scroll

Tuning pegs

Neck

Fingerboard

Strings

Ribs

Bridge

Sound hole

Belly

Tailpiece

Chin rest

BEDRICH SMETANA (1824-1884) *Bohemia*
At some stage in the musical history of each country there is a composer who manages to establish a 'national' kind of classical music. This often comes at the same time as these countries are getting their political freedom. The composers use the folk tunes of their nations to give their works the special, unmistakable flavour. Smetana was the man who did this for Bohemia, the country now known as Czechoslovakia, at a time when they were trying to free themselves from the Austro-Hungarian Empire which had been in control for a long time. In his great orchestral work *Ma Vlast* (My Country) he paints an unforgettable picture of Bohemia while his lively opera *The Bartered Bride* somehow manages to express the spirit of the Czech people.

Perfection was achieved by experiment, and although they kept much of their art a secret, later craftsmen have been able to make copies of these famous violins. The perfect shape and proportion was naturally of prime importance, but tone was also affected by the choice of wood, the mixing of the varnishes, and the placing of the *bridge* and the soundpost which is inside the instrument, supporting the weight of the bridge and the tension of the strings. No better instruments have ever been made than those produced by the Italian mastercraftsmen and all the great virtuoso violinists try to own one of these fine instruments.

The violin is the highest pitched member of the string family: agile and clear toned, it is the leading instrument of the modern orchestra.

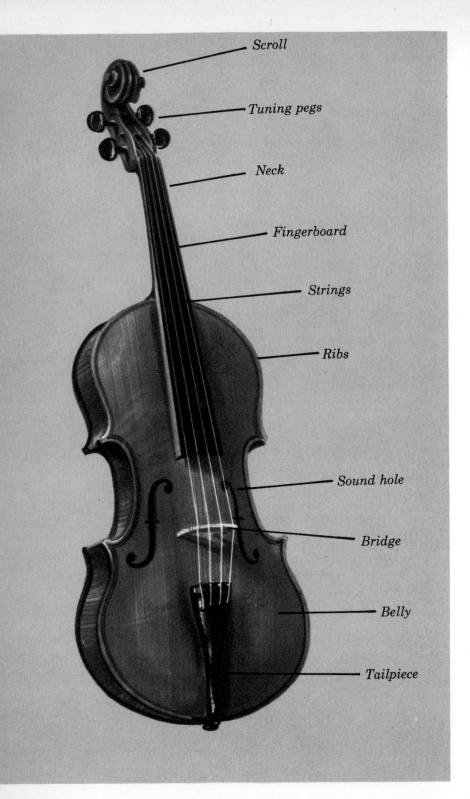

Scroll

Tuning pegs

Neck

Fingerboard

Strings

Ribs

Sound hole

Bridge

Belly

Tailpiece

The viola, a member of the string family, slightly larger than the violin, is a tenor to the violin's soprano: it is mellow toned but less popular as a solo instrument.

The violin is capable of great agility and violinists like to show off their dazzling technique, so most violin concertos and other violin compositions give opportunity for virtuosity to delight the violinist and his audience. Beside playing with the bow and with the fingers, and also *double* and *triple stopping*, the string player has one or two other tricks at his fingertips which composers will occasionally use for special effects, such as playing with the back of the bow – *col legno*. The most commonly used effect is *muting – con sordino*. A mute is a device which dampens down some of the vibrations and softens the sound of the instrument giving a soft and distant effect. In the case of the violin family it is a piece of shaped wood which clamps on to the bridge, lessening the power of the vibrations transmitted through the bridge to the sounding body of the instrument.

The VIOLA is about a fifth larger than the violin and has a slightly richer and foggier tone. Not quite as sparkling as the violin, it is not so popular as a solo instrument, and not a great deal of music has been written especially for it. But it is an essential part of the string quartet and fills in the gap between the violin and the cello range. The violas are most effective in the orchestra with their rather sad and romantic sound.

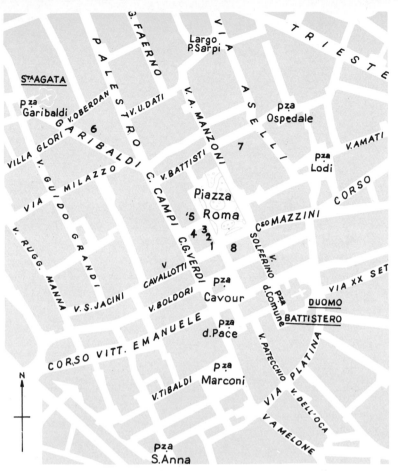

A map of Cremona with the workshops of the most famous violin makers clearly shown:
1. Antonio Stradivari's shop; 2. Carlo Bergonzi's shop; 3. The shop of Joseph Guarneri del Gesu; 4. The shop of Antonio and Hieronymus Amati; 5. Rough location of Lorenzo Storioni and G. B. Ceruti's shop; 6. The home of Francesco Pescaroli; 7. The home and workshop of Gio Maria Cironi; 8. Nicolo Amati's shop.

JOHANN STRAUSS II (1825-1899) *Austria*
Following in the steps of Austrian composers like Schubert and, later, Josef Lanner (1801-1843), and his father the elder Johann Strauss (1804-1849), the younger Strauss wrote a large number of wonderful waltzes which made use of the Viennese dance in 3/4 time as no composer has done before or since. They were so good of their kind that they not only became very popular amongst the Viennese, but were much admired by serious composers like Wagner and Brahms, and soon spread all over the world. *The Blue Danube, Voices of Spring, Tales from the Vienna Woods* will never be forgotten; nor his sparkling operetta *Die Fledermaus* (The Bat) which seems to capture the whole spirit of traditional, gay Vienna.

Two viols – ancestors of the modern violin family.

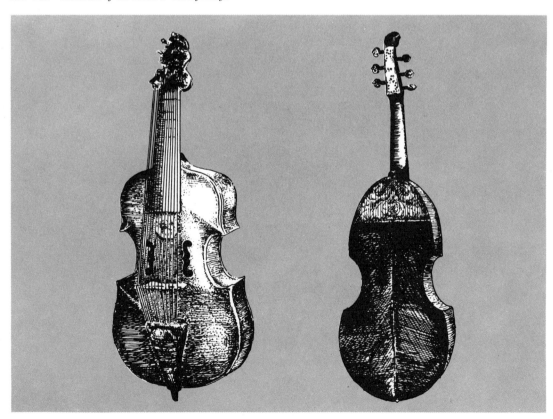

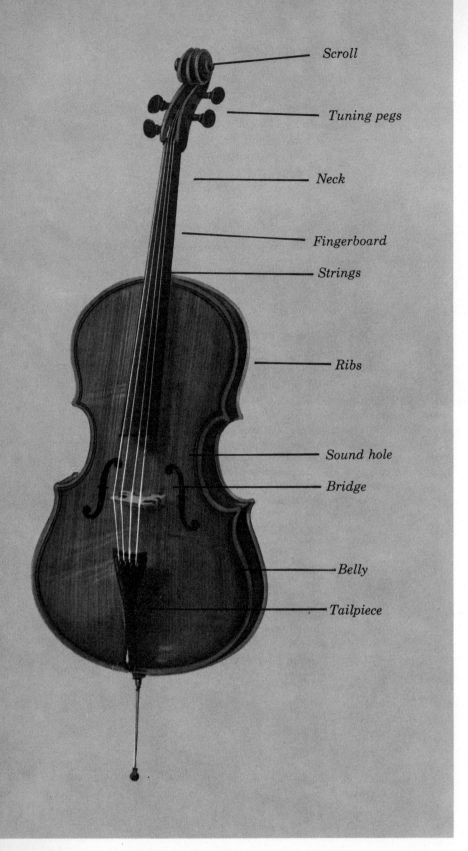

Scroll

Tuning pegs

Neck

Fingerboard

Strings

Ribs

Sound hole

Bridge

Belly

Tailpiece

The cello is a large member of the violin family. Midway in size between the viola and the double-bass, it might be considered the baritone of the string section. The cello is always played in a seated position.

The VIOLONCELLO or CELLO, larger still and with a beautifully rich tone, does not pretend to be as agile as a violin but is still capable of remarkable virtuosity. It charms us with its warm and mellow voice. Composers have been greatly attracted by the amenable tones of this instrument and there is a great deal of music written for it. If the repertoire is not as great as the violins this is partly because there are fewer cello virtuosos and because it did not become popular as a solo instrument until Beethoven's time. Since then remarkable players like Pablo Casals have made it a very popular instrument. The direct ancestor of the cello was the *viola da gamba*.

The DOUBLE-BASS (which still looks most like a viol with its sloping shoulders and flat back) is so deep in tone that it is rarely used as a solo instrument, except in a tongue-in-cheek sort of way. It provides the deeper orchestral colouring that we so much like to hear. The orchestra would sound very thin indeed without its double-basses. It is played pizzicato far more than the other stringed instruments, especially in jazz groups and dance bands.

The double-bass (below). The largest member of the string family, and, in shape, the one that shows most clearly the ancestry of the viol. Always played in an upright position (see bottom right).

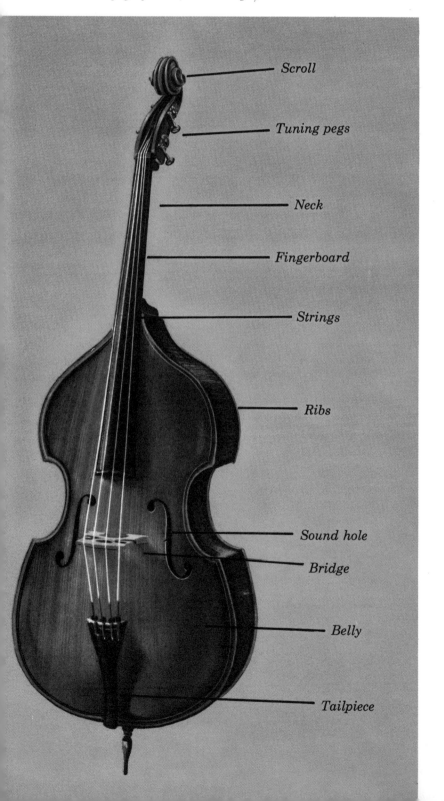

Scroll

Tuning pegs

Neck

Fingerboard

Strings

Ribs

Sound hole

Bridge

Belly

Tailpiece

JOHANNES BRAHMS (1833-1897) *Germany*
To many people Brahms seems to be the typical, serious, weighty German composer, the writer of four big symphonies and two massive piano concertos, some rather serious songs and some solid piano and chamber music. Perhaps the most popular orchestral work that he wrote is the beautiful *Variations on the St. Anthony Chorale.* But he had a light-hearted side as well (he was a great admirer of Johann Strauss), and wrote some very jolly vocal *Liebeslieder* waltzes and the tuneful Waltzes and Hungarian dances, both of which were originally written as piano duets. If his work at first seems rather complicated and heavy he proves, as you get to know him, a warm-hearted and likeable composer.

Violin Concertos and Other Works for Violin

BACH:
Violin concerto in A minor (1717-23)
Violin concerto in E (1717-23)
Concerto for 2 violins in D minor (1717-23)
Sonatas and partitas for solo violin

BARTOK:
Violin concerto No. 2 (1939)

BEETHOVEN:
Romances for violin & orchestra, Op. 40 & Op. 50 (1802)
Violin sonata in A major, Op. 47 'Kreutzer' (1802)
Violin concerto in D, Op. 61 (1806)

BRAHMS:
Violin concerto in D, Op. 77 (1878)
Violin sonata in G major, Op. 78 (1879)

LALO:
Symphonie espagnole, Op. 21 (1873)

MENDELSSOHN:
Violin concerto in E minor, Op. 64 (1844)

MOZART:
Violin concertos — No. 1 in B flat, K207 (1775);
No. 2 in D, K211 (1775); No. 3 in G, K216 (1775);
No. 4 in D, K218 (1775); No. 5 in A, K219 (1775).

PAGANINI:
Caprices, Op. 1 (1804)
Violin concerto No. 1 in E flat (or D), Op. 6 (1805)
Violin concerto No. 2 in B minor, Op. 7 (1805)

SAINT-SAËNS:
Introduction & Rondo capriccioso, Op. 28 (1870)
Havanaise, Op. 83 (1890)

SIBELIUS:
Violin concerto in D minor, Op. 47 (1903/5)

STRAVINSKY:
Violin concerto in D (1931)

TCHAIKOVSKY:
Violin concerto in D, Op. 35 (1878)

VAUGHAN WILLIAMS:
The lark ascending (1914)

A painting of a young woman in a happy mood with a violin, by the Dutch artist Gerard van Honthorst (1590-1656).

Viola Concertos and Other Works for Viola

BERLIOZ:
Symphony 'Harold in Italy' (1834)

HINDEMITH:
Viola concerto 'Der Schwanendreher' (1935)

WALTON:
Viola concerto in A minor (1929)

Cello Concertos and Other Music for Cello

BACH:
Suites for solo cello (BWV1007/12) (1720)

BEETHOVEN:
Variations on 'See the Conquering Hero' in G (1796)

Cello sonatas – No. 1 in F, Op. 5, No. 1 (1796);
No. 2 in G minor, Op. 5, No. 2 (1796);
No. 3 in A, Op. 69 (1808); No. 4 in C, Op. 102, No. 1 (1815);
No. 5 in D, Op. 102, No. 2 (1815).

BOCCHERINI: Cello concerto in B flat (c. 1790)

BRAHMS: Cello sonata in E minor, Op. 38 (1865)
                Concerto for violin & cello in A minor, Op. 102 (1888)

BRUCH: Kol Nidrei, Op. 47 (1880)

CHOPIN: Cello sonata in G minor, Op. 65 (1845-6)

DVOŘÁK: Cello concerto in B minor, Op. 104 (1895)

ELGAR: Cello concerto in E minor, Op. 85 (1919)

GRIEG: Cello sonata in A minor (1882)

HAYDN: Cello concerto in D, Op. 101 (1783)

KODALY: Cello sonata, Op. 4 (1910) Sonata for solo cello, Op. 8 (1915)

PROKOFIEV: Cello sonata in C, Op. 119 (1949)
                Cello concerto (symphony for cello) (1935-8)

SAINT-SAËNS: The Swan *from* Carnaval des Animaux (1886)

SCHUMANN: Cello concerto in A minor, Op. 129 (1850)

SHOSTAKOVITCH: Cello concerto No. 1 in E flat, Op. 107 (1959)

R. STRAUSS: Don Quixote (1897)

TCHAIKOVSKY: Rococo variations for cello & orchestra, Op. 33 (1876)

VILLA-LOBOS: Bachianas Brasileiras, No. 5 (1945)

WALTON: Cello concerto (1957)

PETER TCHAIKOVSKY (1840-1893) *Russia*
Tchaikovsky, the first great Russian composer, can possibly be fairly described as the most popular composer of all time. He pleases so many people by the rich and dramatic sound that he achieved in his writing for the orchestra and by the wonderful, unforgettable melodies that occur in all his works. Among Tchaikovsky's best-loved works are the last three of his six symphonies, the Piano concerto No. 1, the Violin concerto, the fantasy-overture *Romeo and Juliet*, and the music he wrote for three great ballets, *Swan Lake*, *The Sleeping Beauty* and *The Nutcracker*. He also wrote several fine operas, including *Eugene Onegin*.

Two musicians play on the bowed lute to provide music at a wedding. Detail from 'The Wedding at Cana' by Veronese.

Woodwind Instruments

So-called because they are mainly (but not always) constructed of wood, as distinct from the brass instruments which are all metal.

The FLUTE and PICCOLO are the simplest wind instruments used in the orchestra. They are a development of the *recorder* family, the simple penny-whistle type of instrument in which the air is made to vibrate in a tube by blowing through a shaped mouth-piece and the length of the tube is varied by opening or closing holes cut along its length. It was found that the instrument was easier to manipulate if it was blown through a hole in the side and could be held horizontally. Blowing over this *embouchure* hole gives the flute its typical breathy sound. Mechanical keys were added, as in all wind instruments, to give better results than could be achieved by fingertips and to save awkward stretches by the fingers – hence more flexibility. The bottom note of the modern flute is middle C though it plays most naturally from the D and has a liking for keys which have sharps in them. The first octave from D up to the next D is obtained by blowing the flute in a natural, relaxed way. The next octave upward is obtained by over-blowing, that is to say, blowing a little harder and altering the angle of the instrument a little but using the keys in the same way. A further octave upwards is achieved by even harder blowing. So a flute has a useful range of about three octaves. It will be easily understood that the chief difficulty in playing a flute is the control of the breath, for it is very easy to blow a note an octave higher than intended. Although most flutes are made of wood, some players prefer them made of metal, and silver has always been a favourite material.

The piccolo, its name simply meaning small, is a tinier version of the flute, about half its length, and sounding an octave higher. The technique of playing it is exactly the same although the higher notes are rather more difficult to play. It produces a very bright sound easily heard above a full orchestra, but should not be over-used. Most piccolos are made of metal.

A young student of the flute demonstrates the correct method of holding it, and the difficult blowing technique, which controls the octave at which it sounds.

The Flute. A member of the woodwind group that has no reed, the sound being produced by blowing across an aperture, producing a slightly husky sound (see above).

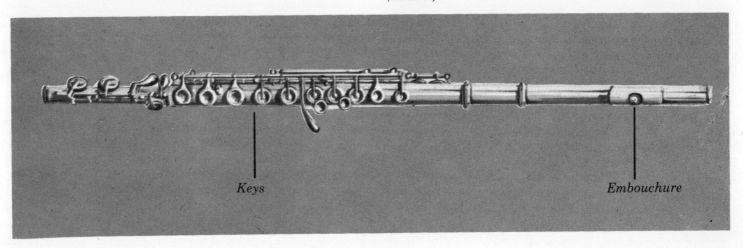

Keys   *Embouchure*

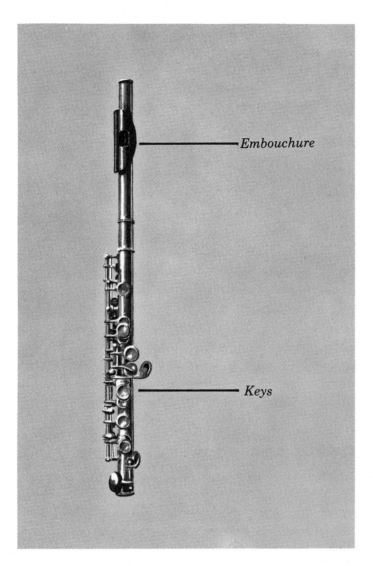

Embouchure

Keys

The Piccolo. A member of the woodwind family, the younger brother to the flute, constructed in exactly the same way, but much smaller and giving much higher notes.

ANTONIN DVOŘÁK (1841-1904) *Bohemia*
While Smetana became the 'national' composer of Czechoslovakia, Dvořák eventually became their great composer, the only one with a big list of symphonies, concertos and other orchestral works to his credit. Dvořák was, in fact, more 'international' in his work, for though his music is full of Czech dances and melodies he also shows clearly in his work that he was very interested in what other European composers, such as Brahms and Wagner, were doing – and he often copied their style of writing. But by the time he wrote his last great symphonies he had found his own clear style. The *Slavonic Dances* are most Bohemian of all his works. After a visit to America he wrote his famous '*New World*' symphony. His Cello Concerto is one of the greatest works ever written for that instrument. He also wrote much fine chamber music.

A young piccolo player shows how this small instrument is held and played.

The next group of instruments employ the same principle of a long tube with holes down its length, operated by metal keys so placed that they lie within easy reach of the fingers, and can open and close holes far beyond the normal hand's stretch. But the air in the tube is made to vibrate by blowing past a reed. The principle of this is that a flexible piece of reed, usually of a light wood, is lying against a flat surface. As the player blows, the reed is lifted up but immediately returns because it has been forced from its natural position. This happens very rapidly and sets up a sort of

buzzing vibration which you might be more familiar with in a mouth-organ, although in that case the reeds are made of thin metal.

The CLARINET, descended from an instrument called the *chalumeau*, is a straight tube with a wider opening at its bottom end, called, as in all wind instruments, the *bell*. It is about two feet long, made in several joinable sections for convenience in carrying, generally of wood or ebonite. Nowadays it has about thirteen keys. The mouth-piece is generally made of wood, sometimes metal, and it uses a single reed, made of carefully thinned cane held on to its flat bed or *table* by a metal strip with an adjusting screw. Its range covers the middle notes of the piano, that is from E below middle C to about C some 3½ octaves higher. Like the flautist, the clarinettist must overblow to reach his higher notes. The clarinet is the first *transposing* instrument we have met. Clarinets are either B flat or A instruments. This we will come across several times in the wind department. We need not go into complicated reasons except to say that it is dictated by the physical nature of the instrument. What happens in practical terms is that when a B flat clarinet plays a bottom E, for example, the sound it produces is the D below it. Therefore, in order to get the clarinet to play an E, the composer must write an F. In other words, he has to write for the instrument in a key one tone higher than he does for the non-transposing instruments, such as the violin family. So you will notice in most scores that the parts are written in several keys – an extra headache for the orchestrator, but one which, through custom, has been accepted as one of the hazards of musical composition.

The clarinet is the most agile of the woodwind and is most frequently used as a solo instrument. Similar in appearance to the oboe, it uses a single reed, and produces a clearer note.

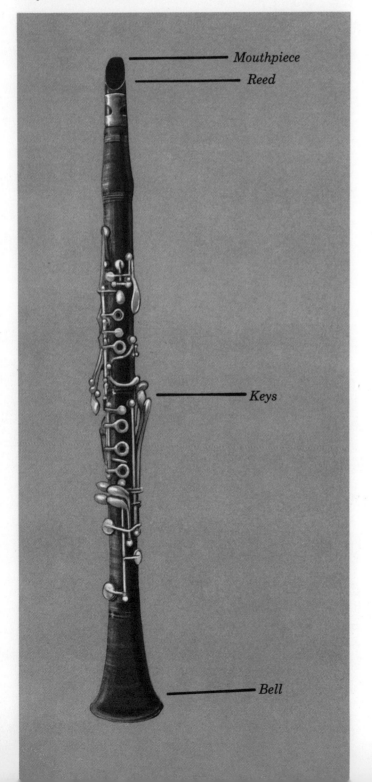

Mouthpiece

Reed

Keys

Bell

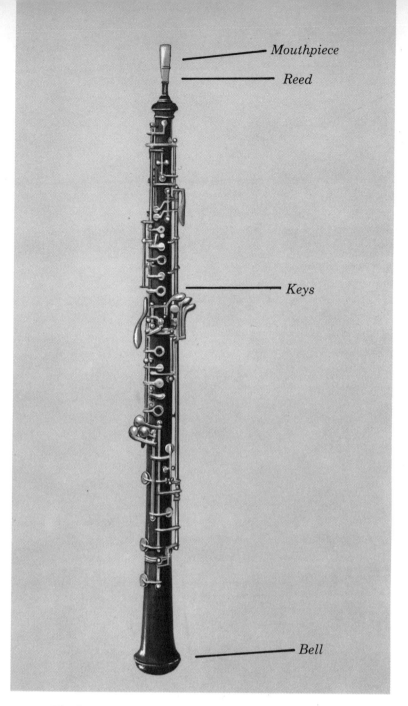

Mouthpiece
Reed

Keys

Bell

The oboe (see below).

EDVARD GRIEG (1853-1907) *Norway*
Norway's national composer was a small, quiet man who lived a simple life and wrote what sometimes seemed rather old-fashioned music. He hardly ever wrote anything very big – light, descriptive pieces for the piano, wistful little songs and some very attractive music to go with a production of a strange play by Ibsen called *Peer Gynt*. Theatre producers of today do not find his music suited to the play, but it will always be remembered for its own sake. Much of Grieg's work is based on traditional Norwegian music. His one big work is the Piano Concerto which, as it has become one of the most popular compositions of all time, makes us wonder why he did not write more like it.

An oboe player.

Note: In Haydn's day instruments in C were rather commoner. The clarinet in C has now gone out of fashion, but you will notice in our score that the possible transposing instruments are all in C. There is also a BASS CLARINET in fairly common use.

The OBOE is similar in appearance to the clarinet with one noticeable difference – at the upper end it has a short length of metal tubing between the main wooden, or ebonite, body of the instrument and the mouth-piece. At the top of this the reeds are fitted, for the oboe has a double-reed, two pieces of cane bound together and which vibrate together when the musician blows the instrument.

The oboe is a very ancient instrument, also known as the *hautboy*, from the French, and descended from an ancestor called the *schalmey*. It has a very reedy, rather nasal tone, compared to the clarinet's smoother sound. Its range is from the B flat below middle C to 2½ octaves above. All these instrumental ranges are approximate and depend on the ability of the musician. What may be thought of as an alto or contralto oboe with a slightly lower compass of sound is the *English horn* or COR ANGLAIS. It is practically the same as the oboe, slightly longer and with a distinctive globular bell, and has more or less the same fingering and technique.

The BASSOON is a kind of bass oboe with a similar double reed, but being a lower-pitched instrument it needs a greater length to produce its lower notes. If the bassoon was straight it would be about six feet long so it doubles back on itself with a U-shaped bend in the bore and manages to reduce its length to about 4 feet. The player holds the instrument in front of him with the small tube, or crook, coming out of the instrument at right angles to the main body. The range is from the B flat below the bass stave to the E flat about 2½ octaves above. There is also a double or CONTRA-BASSOON of greater size and lower pitch used in the modern orchestra.

The cor anglais being played.

The cor anglais is a member of the woodwind section and is a tenor oboe with a double reed and a distinctive globed bell.

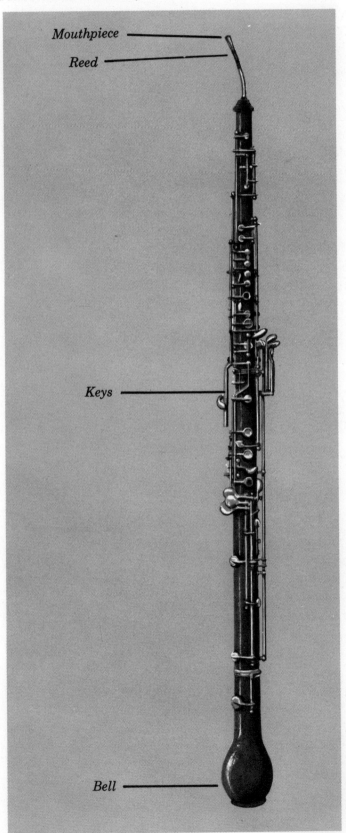

Mouthpiece

Reed

Keys

Bell

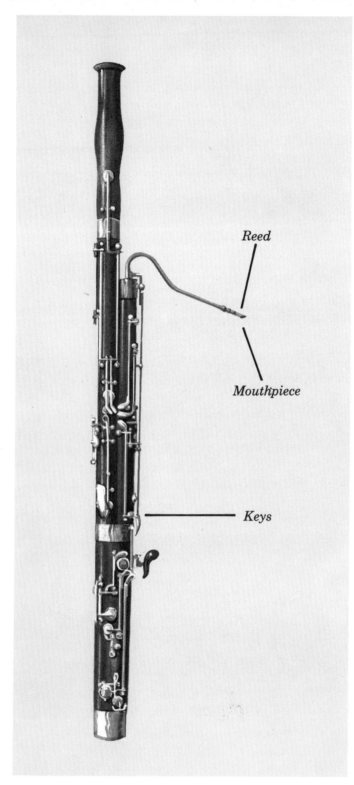

Reed

Mouthpiece

Keys

The bassoon is an instrument of the woodwind family with a double reed and conical bore. Generally, it is thought of as a bass oboe but it has a rather different tone quality.

EDWARD ELGAR (1857-1934) *England*
After Purcell, England had many fine composers but (as we have pointed out) the great influence of the German Handel seems to have prevented them from finding a truly English way of writing. Elgar was the first, for many generations, to prove himself a really great composer. Much of his music, such as the *Introduction and Allegro for Strings*, the Violin concerto and the Cello concerto, reflects his love of the English countryside. Others of his compositions, like the *Cockaigne Overture* and the two symphonies, express in more general terms the social climate of Edwardian England. But the work that established his reputation, the beautiful *Enigma Variations*, remains his best-loved piece of music.

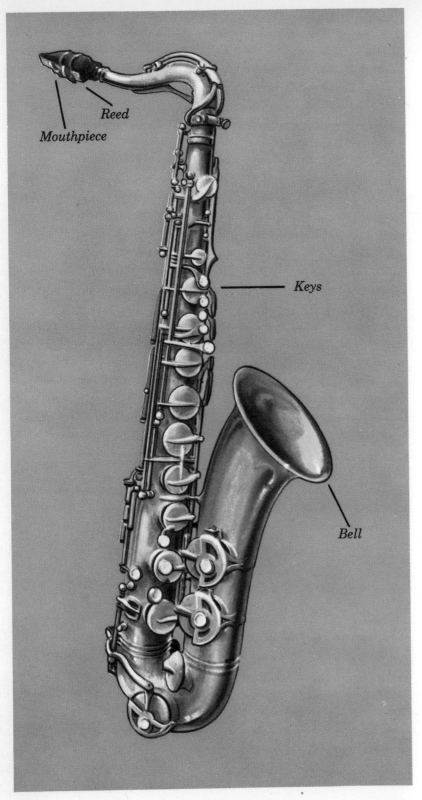

Before we leave the woodwind family we must mention the SAXOPHONES. These well-known instruments, with their familiar S-shape (except the soprano-saxophone which is straight and looks like a large clarinet), occasionally find their way into the modern orchestra, but their rather oily tone has been found more suitable, on the whole, for jazz and popular music. They are fairly recent instruments, invented by Adolphe Sax in 1846, and they are hybrids, being brass (or other metal) instruments in the body, but having clarinet type reeds and keys. The four in main use are the baritone, the tenor, the alto and the soprano saxophone.

The saxophone. A family of hybrid instruments (built of brass but using reeds) invented by Adolphe Sax around 1846. Baritone, tenor, alto, and soprano saxophones are in common use.

Flute Concertos and Works for Flute

CIMAROSA:	Concerto for two flutes in G (1793)
HAYDN:	Flute concerto in D (c. 1765)
MOZART:	Flute concerto No. 1 in G, K313 (1778)
	Flute concerto No. 2 in D, K314 (1778)
	Andante for flute and orchestra in C, K315 (1778)

Flute and harp concerto in C, K299 (1778)
Flute quartets 1-4, K285, K285a, K285b, K298 (1777-8)

NIELSEN: Flute concerto (1926)

WEBER: Trio for flute, cello and piano, Op. 63 (1819)

Clarinet Concertos and Works for Clarinet

BAX: Concerto for clarinet, cor anglais and horn (1949)

BEETHOVEN: Clarinet trio in B flat, Op. 11 (1797)

BRAHMS: Clarinet quintet in B minor, Op. 115 (1891)

COPLAND: Clarinet concerto (1948)

MOZART: Clarinet trio in E flat, K498 (1786)
Clarinet quintet in A, K581 (1789)
Clarinet concerto in A, K622 (1791)

NIELSEN: Clarinet concerto, Op. 57 (1928)

SPOHR: Clarinet concerto No. 1 in C minor, Op. 26 (1812)

STRAVINSKY: Ebony concerto (Clarinet & Jazz orchestra) (1946)

WEBER: Clarinet concerto in F minor, Op. 73 (1811)
Clarinet concerto No. 2 in E flat, Op. 74 (1811)
Clarinet quintet in B flat, Op. 34 (1815)
Duo concertante for clarinet and piano in E flat Op. 48 (1816)

Oboe Concertos and Other Works

BACH: Concerto for Violin, Oboe and strings in D minor (BWV1660)

HANDEL: Concertos for oboe and strings, No. 1 in B flat, No. 2 in B flat, No. 3 in G minor (1740)

HAYDN: Oboe concerto in C (c. 1765)

GUSTAV MAHLER (1860-1911) *Austria*
Mahler was another composer who managed to achieve nine symphonies – we might even consider him as the last of the great symphony writers. Sometimes he is compared to Bruckner but this is simply because they both wrote rather big works. Mahler's are quite different – full of wonderful melodies, some original, some from Austrian folk songs. He loved strong rhythms and, although he was a very serious writer, he also had a great sense of humour. His works are long and rambling, but they are always changing and full of musical surprises. He was also a great conductor and knew how to use the orchestra to good effect.

MOZART: Oboe concerto in D, K314b (1778)
Oboe quartet in F, K370 (1781)

R. STRAUSS: Oboe concerto (1946)

VAUGHAN WILLIAMS: Oboe concerto in A minor (1944)

Bassoon

MOZART: Bassoon concerto in B flat, K191 (1774)
Sonata for bassoon and cello, K292 (1775)

WEBER: Bassoon concerto in F, Op. 75 (1811)
Andante e rondo ongarese in C minor, Op. 35 (1813, originally for viola 1809)

Brass Instruments

As a family the brass instruments were the last to become well-developed virtuoso instruments. Their basic ancestor is the bugle, or the keyless horn, which can simply blow the main harmonic notes of the key in which it is tuned, usually a flat key, F, B flat, or E flat. First of all, extra lengths of tubing were added so that they could play in more than one key, and later keys were added to obtain the other notes of the chromatic scale. In Haydn's time, as we have already noted, brass instruments were still severely limited as to what they could do.

The TRUMPET and its short and fat relation, the CORNET, are the highest pitched members of the brass family. The cornet is more frequently used in brass or military bands than in the symphony orchestra. The sound is produced by setting up a rasping vibration with closed lips into a cup-shaped mouthpiece. In common use now are trumpets in F and B flat. They have a sharp, piercing tone and a range of something over two octaves. There is also a bass-trumpet.

A trumpeter shows clearly how the keys are depressed with the right hand, and the instrument is held with the left.

The trumpet is a high pitched brass instrument with keys, developed from the more primitive bugle.

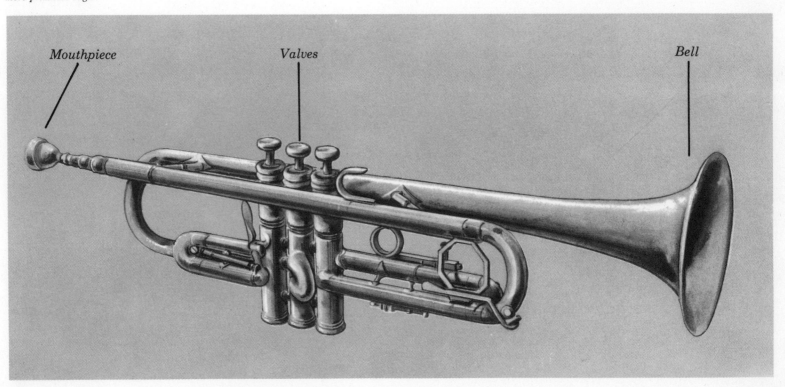

Mouthpiece   *Valves*   *Bell*

The FRENCH HORN is a deeper-pitched instrument than it looks. In fact, its ordinary length of tubing is over seven feet, which is coiled into one and a half circles, and by adding extra *crooks* it can extend itself to over eleven feet. Horns are generally in F, but there are instruments of other pitches more commonly used on the Continent. With three valves, it has a compass from the C above middle C down through three octaves. By inserting his hand in the wide bell of the instrument the player can flatten any played note, and if he is a good player can flatten it accurately by a semitone. Ability to use this technique obviously makes him a more flexible performer. The horn has also a great range of tone from the clear, ringing, challenging note to the far-away, mysterious sound of the muted instrument.

CLAUDE DEBUSSY (1862-1918) *France*
Debussy was a very adventurous composer and a great leader of 20th century music. At the end of the 19th century, composers had begun to feel that the great classical and romantic symphony writers had said all that there was to say in the old forms of music. So Debussy began to explore the possibilities of music that suggested moods and scenes simply through musical sounds – new harmonies and mixtures of instruments and even new scales. When people first heard music like *La Mer* (1904), they were very critical, but it was not long before this and *L'après midi d'un faune* (1894) became popular concert pieces. His chamber music and piano music also seemed very daring at the time, even a piece like *Golliwog's Cakewalk* from the *Children's Corner* suite (1908).

The French horn is a brass instrument with valves, normally pitched in F.

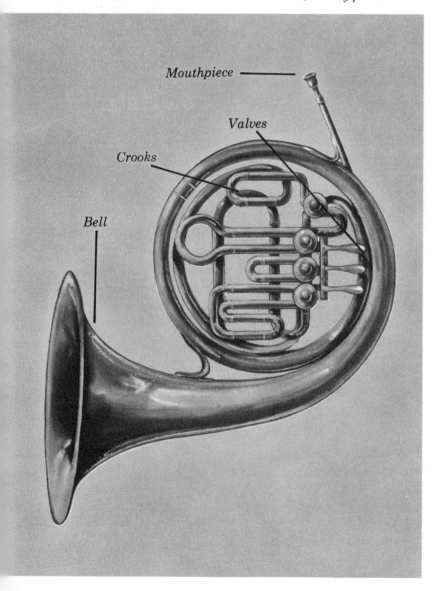

Mouthpiece ————

Valves

Crooks

Bell

The French horn. Note the position of the fingers on the keys and the mouthpiece tight against the lips.

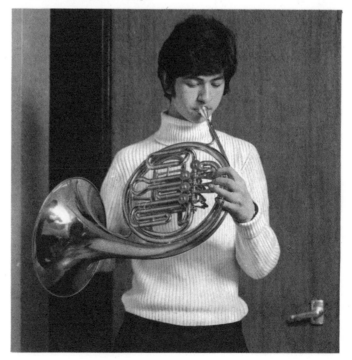

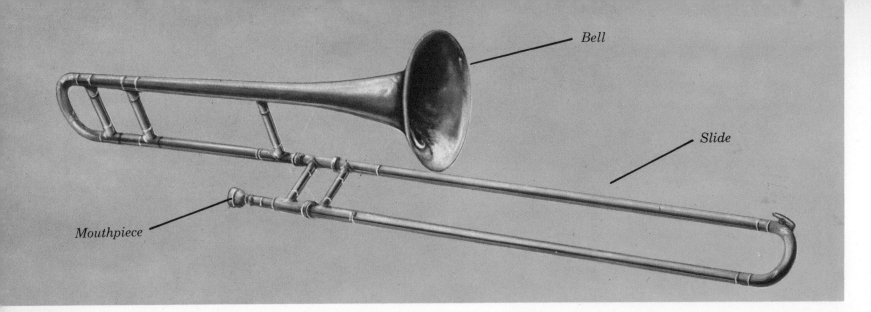

Bell

Slide

Mouthpiece

The TROMBONE is another instrument of ancient lineage and is still much as it was in early times when it was called the *sackbut*. The tenor and the bass trombone are those now in most common use. It has no valves; its long length of tubing, in a long U-shape, is altered by extending or shortening the outer U over two straight lengths of tubing. The player thus has to find his own notes much as the string player does, depending on a good ear. Certain notes being available in more than one position of the slide, it is up to a good player to choose his alternatives. The trombone is usually given an impressive full-throated part in the orchestra but is capable of a very smooth *legato* tone as we know from its use in the jazz and dance-music field.

The trombone is a brass instrument originally known as the 'sackbut', of low pitch and with a unique slide action.

The tuba, the brass band's equivalent of the string bass, is a low pitched instrument of the orchestral brass section.

A trombone player. The right hand moves the slide up and down, while the left holds the instrument to the lips.

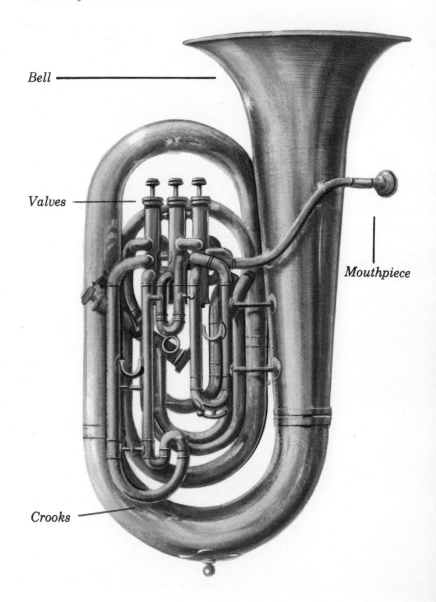

Bell

Valves

Mouthpiece

Crooks

RICHARD STRAUSS (1864-1949) *Germany*
Strauss had a lot of experience as an orchestral player and as a conductor, so it was not surprising that he became one of the most skilled writers for the orchestra. He was not much interested in writing symphonies or sonatas but instead wrote a number of interesting pieces that he called symphonic poems – full of musical portraits and stories suggested by music. *Don Juan* (1888), *Till Eulenspiegel* (1895) and *Don Quixote* (1897) are three of the lively characters that interested him. Rich and varied orchestration was also used in his operas, including *Salomé* by Oscar Wilde which some people found too daring. Although no relation of the other Strausses, Richard loved the Viennese waltz, and filled his opera *Der Rosenkavalier* (1911) with wonderful music in this vein.

Finally, in the brass section of the modern symphony orchestra we should expect to find a TUBA, a large portly instrument, usually played between the player's knees with the bell uppermost. Its thick bore produces very deep notes generally to bolster up the trombone section. It was introduced into the orchestra by Wagner.

Trumpet Concertos, etc.

CLARKE:	Suite in D for trumpets and strings (c. 1700) Trumpet voluntary (1700)
HAYDN:	Trumpet concerto in E flat (1796)
PURCELL:	Trumpet sonata in D (c. 1680–5)
SHOSTAKOVITCH:	Concerto for piano, trumpet and strings, Op. 35 (1933)
VIVALDI:	Concerto for two trumpets in C (1735)

Horn Concertos, etc.

BRITTEN:	Serenade for tenor, horn and strings, Op. 31 (1943)
HAYDN:	Horn concerto No. 1 in D (1762) Horn concerto No. 2 in D (1781)

MOZART:	Horn concerto No. 1 in D, K412 (1782) Horn concerto No. 2 in E flat, K417 (1783) Horn concerto No. 3 in E flat, K447 (1783) Horn concerto No. 4 in E flat, K495 (1786) Horn quintet in E flat, K407 (1782)
R. STRAUSS:	Horn concerto No. 1 in E flat, Op. 11 (1882) Horn concerto No. 2 in E flat (1942)

Tuba

VAUGHAN WILLIAMS:	Concerto for bass tuba in F minor (1954)

Percussion

Used in Haydn's symphony and the central eye-catcher of any symphony orchestra are the TIMPANI (also known as kettle-drums), looking like great copper cauldrons. Their value to the composer is due to the fact that they can be tuned and can thus add harmony and colour to the orchestra as well as a purely percussive effect. They are tuned by tightening the vellum heads, usually in the tonic and dominant notes of the scale of the key in which the music is being played. In our score, for example, they are tuned in C and G. They vary in size, the larger taking the lower note, the smaller the higher notes. In the modern orchestra a vast range of percussion instruments is to be found. These include the SIDE DRUM (or SNARE DRUM), the familiar military instrument which has wires (which are called *snares*) stretched across the lower vellum head to give the distinctive rattling sound; the TENOR DRUM, a larger instrument without snares; and the BASS DRUM which will generally be found in the orchestra with only one vellum head about 3 feet in diameter, whereas the marching bass drum has vellum on both sides and is played with a fine flourish of drumsticks.

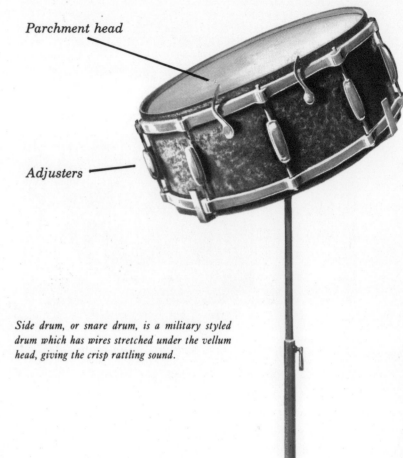

Parchment head

Adjusters

Side drum, or snare drum, is a military styled drum which has wires stretched under the vellum head, giving the crisp rattling sound.

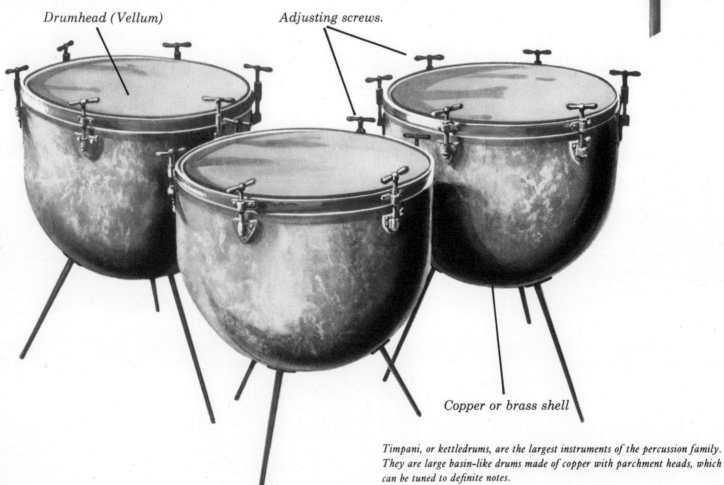

Drumhead (Vellum)

Adjusting screws.

Copper or brass shell

Timpani, or kettledrums, are the largest instruments of the percussion family. They are large basin-like drums made of copper with parchment heads, which can be tuned to definite notes.

Adjusting screws   Parchment head

The tenor drum used for dance band work.

JEAN SIBELIUS (1865-1957) *Finland*
The one great composer produced by the small northern country of Finland, his music is strange and bare, reflecting the cold Arctic climate, and very different from anything else being written in the rest of Europe at the time. In his later years Sibelius liked to lead a lonely life, seeing very few visitors and writing very little new music. Having said all there was to say about the cold landscape of the North in a manner that was at first thought strange and difficult, he quietly retired, while his music, including seven great symphonies, became accepted by the whole world. More easily approachable are some of the shorter descriptive pieces like *The Swan of Tuonela* and *Valse Triste*.

Parchment head

Adjusting screws

The bass drum used for orchestral or dance bands.

Music for Percussion

BARTOK:	Music for strings, percussion and celesta (1936)
CHAVEZ:	Toccata for percussion instruments (1942)
MILHAUD:	Concerto for percussion and small orchestra (1930)

A modern jazz drummer with bass drum, cymbals and snare drum.

Adding their thrilling clashes to the orchestral sound are the CYMBALS, two round brass plates used one in each hand. Occasionally, in the orchestra, the cymbals are hit with a stick or brush – a practice which has become commonplace in jazz and dance orchestras. The TRIANGLE, a piece of metal bent to a triangular shape, adds its pleasant tinkle. Occasional effects are called for from the TAM-TAM or GONG, an Eastern instrument a glorified version of the dinner-gong; the TAMBOURINE, a small one-sided drum with jingling pieces of metal like small cymbals let into the side, which is hit with the hand, rubbed or shaken; the CASTANETS, familiar in Spanish music; and a host of other special effects are obtained from the WOOD BLOCK, SLEIGH BELLS, COWBELL, RATTLE, and so on.

The triangle is a bent bar of metal struck by a metal rod to give a tinkling note.

The tam-tam is another name for the orchestral gong; a percussion instrument of indefinite pitch.

The tambourine is a small one-sided vellum–headed drum struck by the hand, or on the body, which simultaneously sets in motion the small jingling plates let into the side.

Parchment head

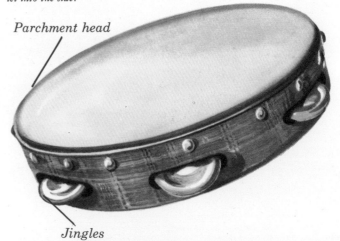

Jingles

The sleigh bell is used mainly for the effect suggested by its name.

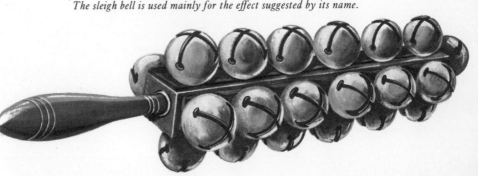

74

A school percussion band playing a variety of instruments.

The castanets are played in pairs, held in the fingers and palm of the hand. Most often associated with the Spanish dance.

The wood block. One of the percussionist's many special effects, giving a crisp boxy sound when hit by the drumsticks.

The cow bell. Originally, the ordinary central European cow bell with the clapper removed, the modern orchestral cow bell is hit by the percussionist to give an atmospheric effect.

SERGEI RACHMANINOV (1873-1943) *Russia*

Rachmaninov was one of the last great virtuoso composers in the Paganini and Liszt tradition. He was a marvellous pianist of great skill and he wrote music of the kind that other virtuoso pianists love to play. He wrote four fine piano concertos, all of which he recorded himself, the very popular one being No. 2. In the 1930s it looked as if Rachmaninov had written all that he could, and the critics said so, but were shown to be very wrong when the composer wrote his most original and striking work of all – the Rhapsody on a Theme of Paganini (1934). The piece that made him famous was his Prelude in C sharp minor and, although he wrote many more short piano pieces during his lifetime, none of them ever became as popular as this composition.

The rattle is used to produce a loud clacking sound.

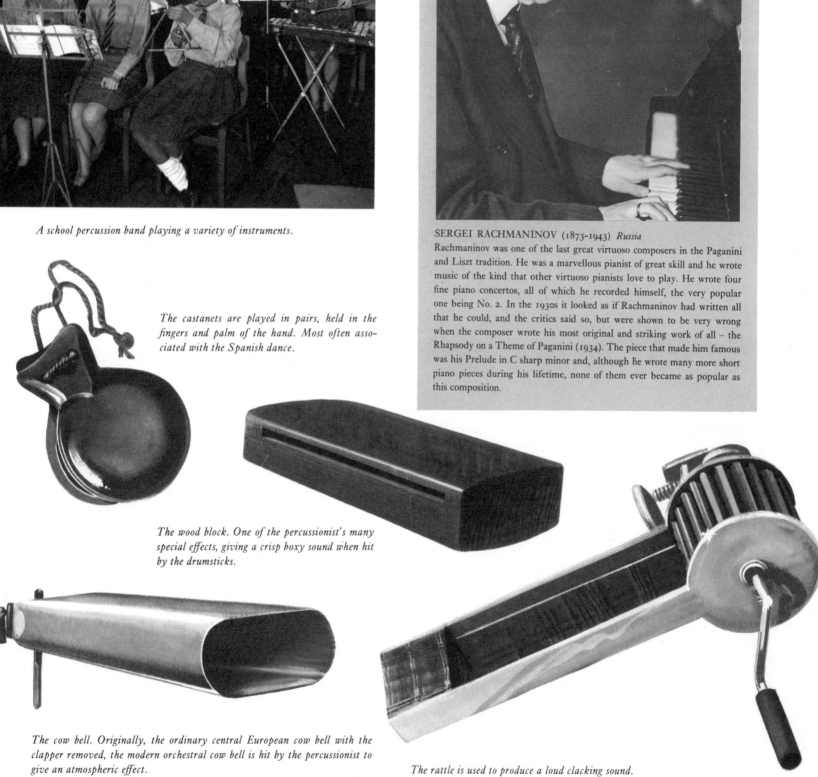

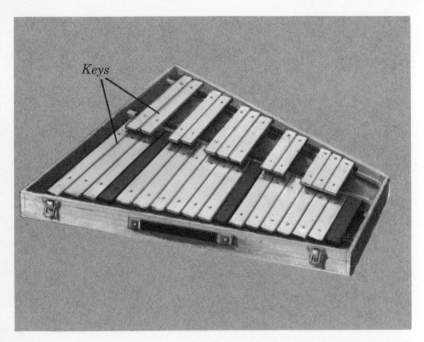

Keys

The glockenspiel is a small portable melodic percussion instrument with tuned bars of metal struck by hammers.

Beside these non-tuned instruments the percussion player will be expected to use a number of tuned percussion instruments such as the GLOCKENSPIEL which has tuned metal bars arranged in two rows like a piano keyboard and is hit with mallets; the XYLOPHONE, a similar instrument with wooden bars; the MARIMBA, a kind of deep-toned xylophone played with soft-headed mallets; the VIBRAPHONE, with bars of metal alloy and tubes under them which can be rapidly opened and closed with little mechanically operated fans to give it, as the name suggests, a vibrating tone; TUBULAR BELLS or CHIMES, a set of metal tubes hung in a frame to give a church bell effect; and HANDBELLS, which are nothing more than a set of clappered bells tuned over an octave or more range.

A young girl playing the glockenspiel.

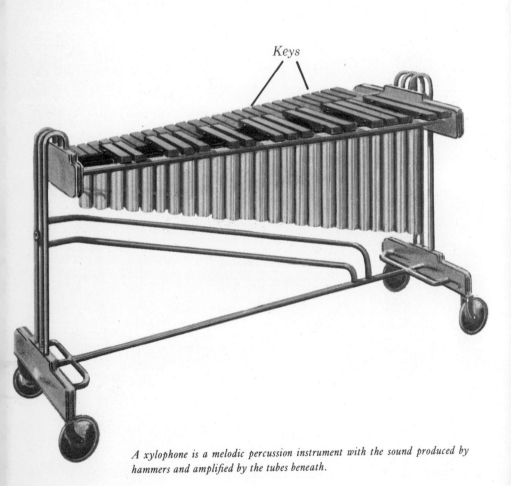

Keys

A xylophone is a melodic percussion instrument with the sound produced by hammers and amplified by the tubes beneath.

76

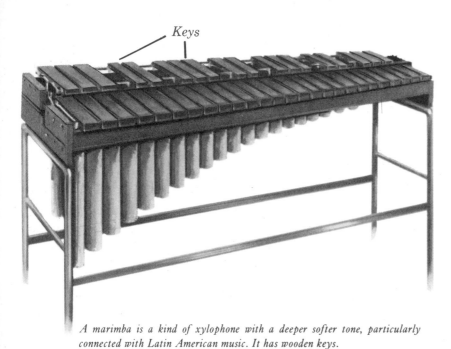

Keys

A marimba is a kind of xylophone with a deeper softer tone, particularly connected with Latin American music. It has wooden keys.

ARNOLD SCHÖNBERG (1874-1951) *Austria*

After several centuries of music written using the system of keys and harmonies and forms established by the great classical composers, Arnold Schönberg and his pupils Webern and Berg invented a new system of composing music that changed everything. It used the twelve notes of the chromatic scale (see page 28) and was in no fixed key. At first it naturally sounded strange and off-putting but, as with all new things, the public gradually got used to it. Younger composers eagerly accepted the new methods and most of the music being written today owes something to Schönberg's ideas. Perhaps the most successful piece, or at least the most acceptable, is his Violin concerto. He also wrote some music in a more traditional manner in his early days such as *Verklärte Nacht.*

The vibraphone player in the Modern Jazz Quartet. The vibraphone is played with two padded sticks to produce a soft muffled tone.

The vibraphone is a modern development of the xylophone, with electrically driven vibratory mechanism which produces a sustained and wavering note.

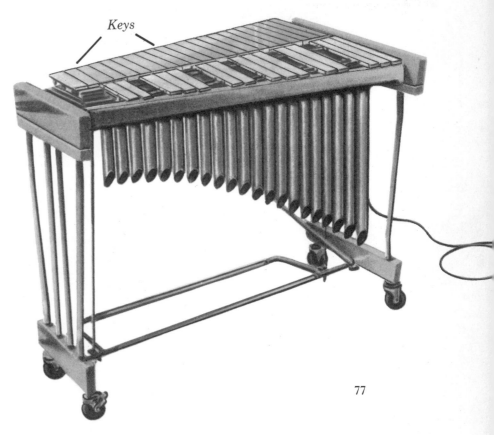

Keys

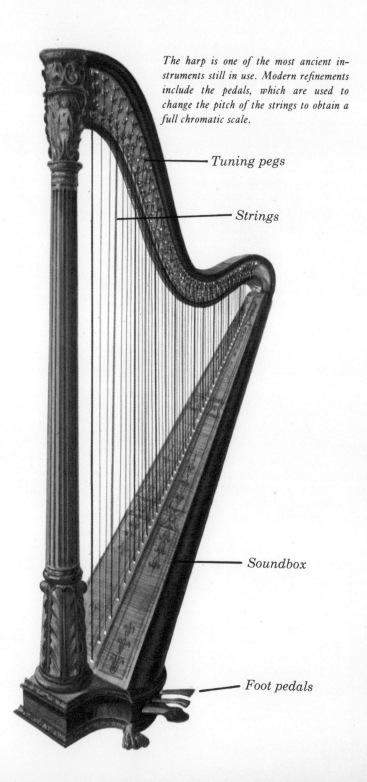

The Harp

Perhaps belonging most logically to the string family, but rather a lone-wolf in the orchestra, is one of the world's most ancient instruments, the HARP, whose history goes nearly as far back as man's. The modern harp is a large instrument, usually played in a seated position, with numerous strings covering some 6½ octaves and pedals by means of which the player can raise their tuning by a semitone or tone and can thus obtain all the notes of the diatonic scale. The strings are plucked by both hands, one either side. Its *arpeggios* and *glissandos* are familiar in works of the 19th century or later; and it is also a wonderful solo instrument.

The harp is one of the most ancient instruments still in use. Modern refinements include the pedals, which are used to change the pitch of the strings to obtain a full chromatic scale.

—— *Tuning pegs*

—— *Strings*

—— *Soundbox*

—— *Foot pedals*

Tubular bells. Part of the percussionist's special effects, they give the sound of chimes.

Handbells are used for special effects and are tuned to a scale.

78

The harpist plays by plucking the strings with hooked fingers, and pressing the pedals (not visible) with her feet.

MAURICE RAVEL (1875-1937) *France*

A most imaginative composer, Maurice Ravel did not write a vast amount of music because he spent so much time trying to write pieces that said what he wanted to say to perfection. Each piece he wrote was a new experiment. His first great success was the ballet *Daphnis et Chloé* which he wrote for Diaghilev's Russian Ballet in 1909. He wrote an opera *L'Heure Espagnole* the following year, and experimented with various rhythms that interested him in such exciting compositions as *Rapsodie Espagnole*, *La Valse* and *Bolero*. His *Piano concerto in G* shows that he was very interested in jazz. But perhaps his most subtle music occurs in his compositions for solo piano, such as the *Sonatine* and *Le Tombeau de Couperin*.

Music for Harp

BOIELDIEU: Harp concerto in C (1795)

HANDEL: Harp concerto in B flat (c. 1745)

MOZART: Flute and harp concerto in C, K299 (1788)

RAVEL: Introduction and allegro for harp, flute, clarinet and string quartet (1906)

REINECKE: Harp concerto in E minor, Op. 182 (c. 1860)

RODRIGO: Concert serenade for harp and orchestra (1954)

SPOHR: Variations for harp, Op. 36 (1815)

Musicians with harp and lute.

79

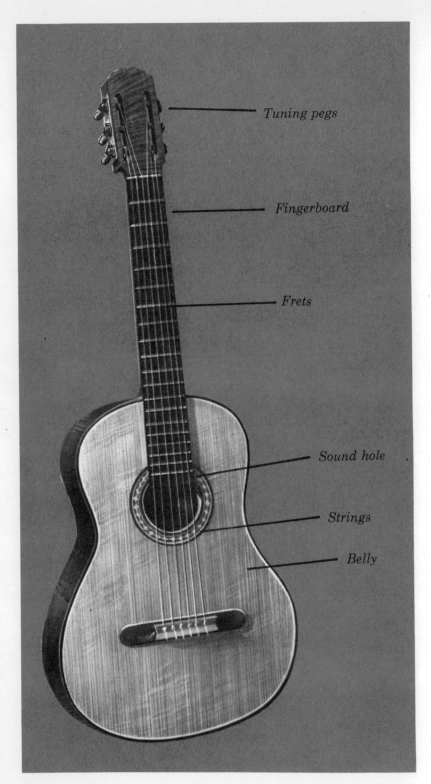

Tuning pegs

Fingerboard

Frets

Sound hole

Strings

Belly

The guitar is a stringed instrument which is plucked, with the position of the notes indicated by the frets let into the fingerboard. Originally associated with Spanish music, it now has world wide popularity.

Before leaving the stringed instruments, mention must be made of the GUITAR, now certainly the most popular of all the 'fretted' instruments – a term which means that instead of having a smooth fingerboard like the violin family, on which the player finds his own fingering position to produce the correct notes, small strips of metal are let into the fingerboard at semitone intervals, and the strings are pressed against these by the fingers. In the instruments of the *lute* family, which are plucked with the fingers or a hard piece of material called a *plectrum*, this also ensures a clearer note without the strings buzzing against the fingerboard, for these instruments have much lower bridges and there is not so much clearance behind the strings. Other fretted instruments are the LUTE itself, the BALALAIKA, the BANJO, the MANDOLIN.

The most popular guitar is the Spanish guitar and naturally enough it is especially associated with Spanish music and the great virtuosos like Segovia. More recently jazz and current trends in folk and popular music have made the guitar the world's favourite instrument. It has a pear-shaped body, a fretted finger-

Joan Baez, a guitarist who specialises in folk music.

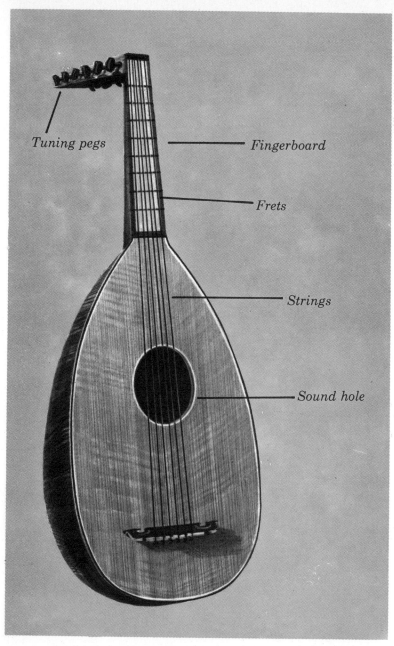

Tuning pegs

Fingerboard

Frets

Strings

Sound hole

The lute is an ancient instrument on which the strings are usually plucked, although there are also bowed lutes.

MANUEL DE FALLA (1876–1946) *Spain*

Spain has not produced many really great composers but Falla is certainly one of them. Like Ravel, he gained his reputation through quite a small list of compositions. There is no mistaking the fact that he was a Spaniard, for his music is full of the traditional warmth and exciting rhythms of that country, based on its flamenco dances and songs. His best-known music comes in the two ballets *El Amor Brujo* (1915) and *The Three-Cornered Hat* (1919), *Nights in the Gardens of Spain* (1916), written in the style of a piano concerto, and in the early work that gained him a reputation as a composer – the opera *La Vida Breve* (1905).

A medieval craftsman in his workshop testing a lute he has just made.

board and most commonly six strings, variously tuned according to taste and nationality. (A twelve-string guitar is often used by many folksingers.) Its exciting and dexterous use in the Spanish *flamenco* (or gypsy folk) music as an accompaniment for singing and dancing has given the guitar a character which is difficult to shake off, so that everything played on it sounds vaguely Spanish. Quite a few composers have used it in one way or another, but its weak tones make it unsuitable as a regular orchestral instrument. The main composers, naturally enough, have been Spaniards. In recent years the electrically amplified guitar has had a great vogue, a trend generally deplored by those who love the sound of this beautiful instrument without its gadgetry.

Music for Guitar

ARNOLD:	Guitar concerto, Op. 67 (1959)
BOCCHERINI:	Quintet No. 3 in E minor, for guitar and strings, Op. 50
CASTELNUOVO-TEDESCO:	Guitar concerto (1939) Guitar quintet, Op. 143 (1950) Platero and I (Suites 1 & 2) (c. 1950) Guitar sonata (Homage to Boccherini) (1933)
DIABELLI:	Trio for flute, viola and guitar (c. 1810)
GIULIANI:	Guitar concerto in A (1808)
PONCE:	Concierto del sur for guitar (1940) Sonata romantica

The banjo is a plucked instrument with a fretted fingerboard, metal strings and vellum sound box, which gives it a very sharp percussive sound.

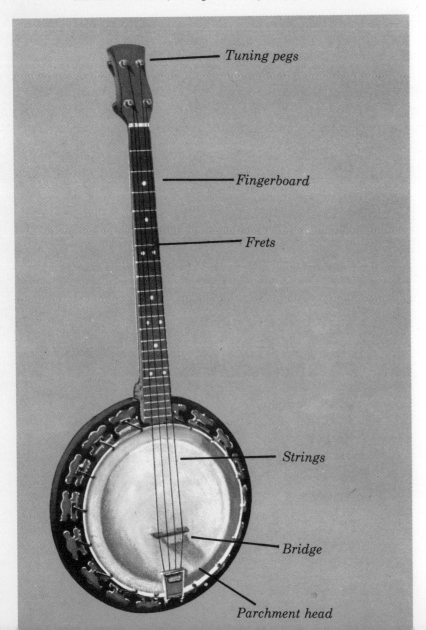

Tuning pegs

Fingerboard

Frets

Strings

Bridge

Parchment head

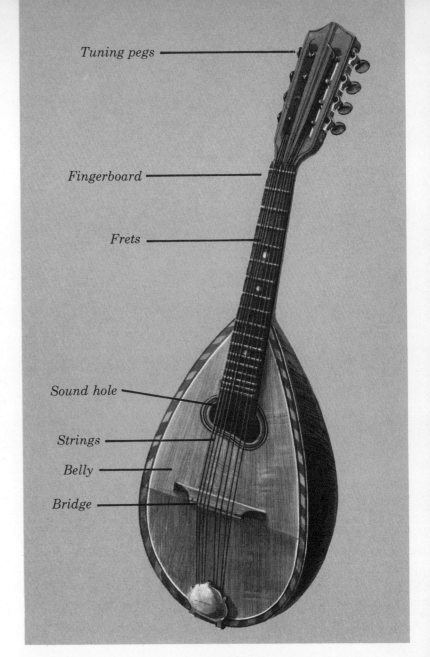

Tuning pegs

Fingerboard

Frets

Sound hole

Strings

Belly

Bridge

The mandolin is a relative of the lute, tuned like the violin and played with a plectrum.

RODRIGO:	Guitar concerto (Concerto de Aranjuez) (1939)
SOR:	Variations on a theme of Mozart, Op. 9 Guitar sonata, Op. 22 20 studies for guitar (c. 1810)
TARREGA:	Recuerdos de la Alhambra (c. 1900)
TORROBA:	Sonata burlesca in F sharp (c. 1930) Sonatina in A (c. 1930)
TURINA:	Fandanguillo, Op. 36 (1926) Hommage à Tarrega Guitar sonata in D minor, Op. 61 (1932)
VILLA-LOBOS:	12 studies for guitar (1929) Preludes for guitar (1940)

Keyboard Instruments

Although the main role in music for the keyboard instruments is as soloists, and they only occasionally find themselves included in the score of entirely orchestral compositions, they very often play with an orchestra, the piano in particular being the most popular 'concerto' instrument, and with chamber groups.

The three most popular keyboard instruments today are the harpsichord, the piano and the organ.

The HARPSICHORD has some modern compositions to its credit but it is chiefly used to interpret music of the 17th and 18th centuries written for it before the piano was developed and largely took its place at the beginning of the 19th century.

It can easily be understood why the piano, with its greater volume of sound, its clearer notes, its easier action and its range of dynamics, should replace the lighter and less varied tones of the harpsichord in the composer's estimation. Indeed, the rather tinny tone of the harpsichord can become a little wearing if it is imposed for too long.

Nevertheless, the harpsichord has a charm of its own and it cannot be satisfactorily replaced by the piano when playing music written during the period of its heyday. The harpsichord

The harpsichord is a keyboard instrument with sound produced by the mechanism plucking the strings. It dates from the early 16th century. The action (see right) is described in the next column.

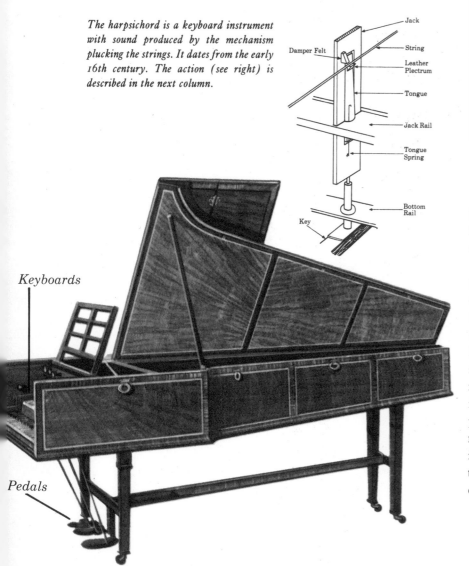

Keyboards

Pedals

BÉLA BARTÓK (1881-1945) *Hungary*
The gypsy melodies and the typical rhythms of Hungarian music have influenced composers far beyond the country's boundaries. But we tend to forget that Liszt was a Hungarian because his music was not particularly nationalistic. It was not until Bartók and Zoltán Kodály began to explore the national music of Hungary thoroughly that the world became very much aware that it had produced distinctive composers. As well as writing national music, Bartók was also a modern composer of great originality. Wonderful colours and harmonies are found in works like his *Concerto for Orchestra*, *Divertimento for Strings* and the 3rd piano concerto. However, his most original and profound musical thinking is brought out in his six string quartets, probably the finest group of such works since Beethoven.

is nearer to being a genuine 'stringed' instrument than the piano for the harpsichord strings are plucked whereas the piano strings are hit by hammers.

The harpsichord is generally of the shape of a grand piano, rather slighter in build, and usually has two piano type keyboards, each controlling a different set of *plectra* or quills, one set hard, the other soft. Sometimes there are *stops* (see under *organ*) which can put other sets into action. In the earlier and simpler forms, known sometimes as the *virginal* or the *spinet*, there is only one string to each note; the later harpsichords generally have two or more. When the note is struck a piece of wood, called the jack, is pushed up past or between the string or strings and a protruding piece called the plectrum plucks the string. When the key is released, the jack falls back into position and the plectrum, which is pivoted, is pushed back into a slot in the jack. It can be seen that, because of this sort of action, the player really has little control over the tone of the instrument.

83

Strings

Keyboard

BACH: Harpsichord concertos (BWV1052-1058)

Concertos for 2 harpsichords (BWV 1060-2)

Goldberg variations (BWV 988)

Forty-eight Preludes and Fugues (BWV 846-93)

FALLA: Concerto for harpsichord, flute, oboe, clarinet, violin and cello (1926)

POULENC: Concert champêtre for harpsichord and orchestra (1928)

SCARLATTI: Numerous sonatas

The spinet is an instrument with a similar action to the harpsichord but rather lighter in tone.

The piano is a keyboard instrument with the sound produced by felt-tipped hammers striking metal strings. Developed at the beginning of the 18th century.

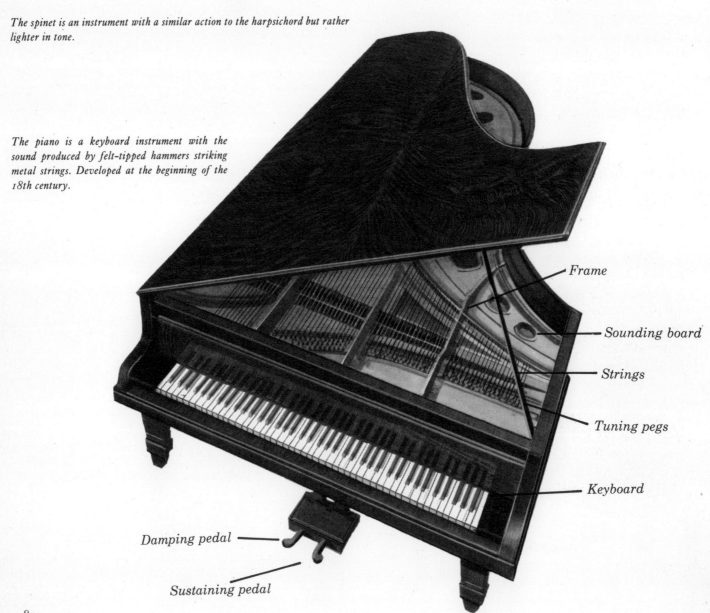

Frame

Sounding board

Strings

Tuning pegs

Keyboard

Damping pedal

Sustaining pedal

84

POULENC:	Concerto in D minor for two pianos (1932)

SERGE PROKOFIEV (1891-1953) *Russia*
The most attractive element in Prokofiev's music is its humour and wit. He never deserted the old musical traditions and you could always guess that he was a Russian by the flavour of his music, except perhaps in the *Classical* symphony which is a deliberate attempt to parody old styles in modern dress. Most typical of Prokofiev are the rich, Russian colours of *The Love of Three Oranges* and *Lieutenant Kije*. His *Peter and the Wolf* is the most successful of all the musical pieces written especially for children. Not all Prokofiev's music is so easy to listen to, but it generally keeps to the Soviet idea that music should be for everyone.

PROKOFIEV:	Piano concerto No. 1 in D flat, Op. 10 (1911) Piano concerto No. 2 in G, Op. 16 (1913) Piano concerto No. 3 in C, Op. 26 (1921) Piano concerto No. 4, Op. 53, for the left hand (1931) Piano concerto No. 5 in G, Op. 55 (1932) 9 Piano sonatas
RACHMANINOV:	Piano concerto No. 1 in F sharp minor, Op. 1 (1890-1) Piano concerto No. 2 in C minor, Op. 18 (1902) Piano concerto No. 3 in D minor, Op. 30 (1909) Piano concerto No. 4 in G minor, Op. 40 (1927) Rhapsody on a theme of Paganini, Op. 43 (1934) 24 Preludes, Op. 3, Op. 23 and Op. 32
RAVEL:	Sonatine (1905) Gaspard de la Nuit (1908) Valses nobles et sentimentales (1911) Le Tombeau de Couperin (1917) Piano concerto in G (1931) Piano concerto for left hand (1931)
SAINT-SAËNS:	Piano concerto No. 2 in G minor, Op. 22 (1868)
SCHUBERT:	Piano quintet in A, D667, 'The Trout' (1819) 21 Piano sonatas 2 sets of Impromptus Op. 90 & Op. 142 Moments musicaux
SCHUMANN:	Carnaval, Op. 9 (1834-5) Kinderscenen, Op. 15 (1838) Arabesque in C, Op. 18 (1839) Piano concerto in A minor, Op. 54 (1845) Piano quintet in E flat, Op. 44 (1842) Waldscenen, Op. 82 (1848-9) etc.

SHOSTAKOVITCH:	Piano concerto No. 2, Op. 101 (1922) Piano quintet, Op. 57 (1940)
STRAVINSKY:	Capriccio for piano and orchestra (1929) Concerto for piano and wind instruments (1931)
TCHAIKOVSKY:	Piano concerto No. 1 in B flat minor, Op. 23 (1875) The seasons, Op. 37 (1876)
WEBER:	Invitation to the dance in D flat, Op. 65 (1819)

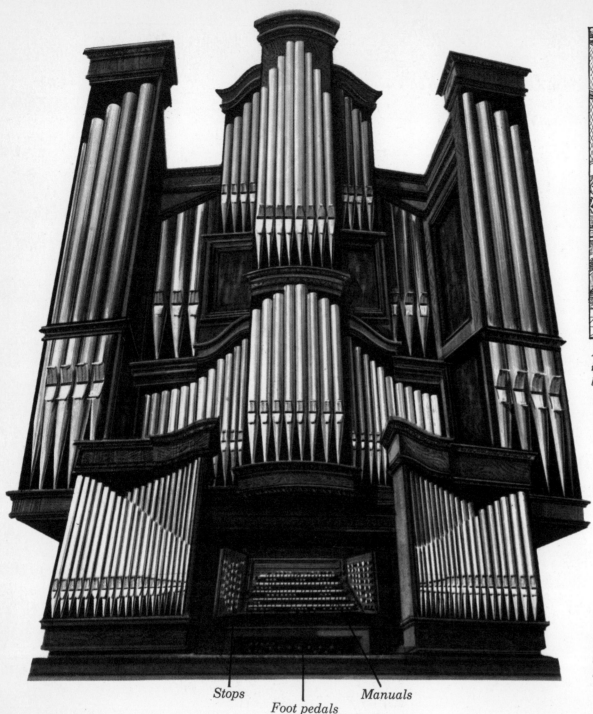

A small portable 15th century organ. The man is playing the notes while the woman works the bellows. Note the dog's expression!

Stops

Foot pedals

Manuals

The organ is a complex keyboard instrument, with the sound produced by air being pumped through pipes of varying lengths and diameter.

Finally the ORGAN. At a time when it was not rivalled by the large symphony orchestra, the organ was considered to be 'the king of instruments'. After the time of Johann Sebastian Bach (1685-1750), however, very few of the great composers spent much time on writing organ music and since that time it has been mainly associated with church music.

Developing from the small *portative* or portable organ and the rather noisy instruments made by the Greeks and Romans, then through the small church organs of the baroque period, the organ gradually became a vast, tremendously expensive and completely immobile instrument blended into the decorative schemes of a few large concert-halls and found in varying degrees of splendour in churches and cathedrals. The modern organ is electrically operated but basically it has not changed much over the last two thousand years. A minority of music-lovers enjoy listening to organ music on its own, but most people prefer its grandiose contribution to large choral works and when it is played in conjunction with an orchestra.

Most of the organ's expanse is made up of the rows of large pipes which are usually remotely controlled by the keyboard.

The organ is, in fact, a mechanical wind band. From the piano styled keyboard, called the *manual* (usually, two or three are needed to operate all the various combinations of pipes found in a modern organ), and a foot-operated keyboard made up of large pedals, it produces its sound by allowing air, pumped mechanically or by hand, to blow through single pipes or sets of pipes. The pipes can be operated singly by the depression of one key, or they can be linked to play in octaves or in harmony. The pipes are split into groups with different tone qualities, each of which is allotted to a manual, usually from two to five (according to the size of the instrument) and these groups have names like *Great, Swell, Choir, Solo* and *Echo*, and a bass group is connected to the pedals. Various other sets of pipes, some designed to give sounds in imitation of other instruments, are brought into action by pulling out knobs, called *stops*, which are ranged on either side of the manual with names like *Flute, Clarinet, Oboe* and *Trumpet*. The whole array of manuals and stops is called the *console*. There are two kinds of pipes in an organ, a simple 'penny-whistle' kind called a *flue-pipe*, and pipes with vibrating reeds called *reed-pipes*. It is possible, by using a *Mixture* stop, to play a chord of simple harmonics by depressing a single key which helps to give the organ its full and lustrous sound. The normal organ is referred to as a *pipe-organ*. There are also *electronic* organs nowadays which have a different tone quality altogether.

The organ of St. Paul's Cathedral. The four manuals and rows of stops are clearly visible.

DIMITRI SHOSTAKOVITCH (b. 1906) *Russia*
Some of the most universally enjoyable music in recent years has come from Russia, and Dimitri Shostakovitch has written music which is very original, and most exciting as well as being very Russian. Like Prokofiev, Shostakovitch is a user of traditional forms, but has proved that you do not need to throw away old styles in order to produce something new. Among his many orchestral compositions the 5th and 10th symphonies and the 1st Cello concerto have won wide international acclaim.

Organ Music

Beside the masses of organ music written by specialist church composers such as J. S. Bach, Buxtehude, Dupré, Frescobaldi, Widor, we list the following of secular interest:

BRITTEN:	Prelude and fugue on a theme of Vittoria (1947)
HANDEL:	Organ concertos (3 sets of 6)
MAHLER:	Symphony No. 8 in E flat (1908)
MOZART:	Organ concertos (Sonata de Chiesa) (1767-80)
POULENC:	Concerto in G for organ, strings and timpani (1938)
PURCELL:	Various works
SAINT-SAËNS:	Symphony No. 3 in C minor, Op. 78 (1886)

Some Well-Known Symphonies and Their Composers

BEETHOVEN:
Symphony No. 1 in C, Op. 21 (1800)
Symphony No. 2 in D, Op. 36 (1802)
Symphony No. 3 in E flat, Op. 55 'Eroica' (1803)
Symphony No. 4 in B flat, Op. 60 (1806)
Symphony No. 5 in C minor, Op. 67 (1807)
Symphony No. 6 in F, Op. 68 'Pastoral' (1807/8)
Symphony No. 7 in A, Op. 92 (1812)
Symphony No. 8 in F, Op. 93 (1812)
Symphony No. 9 in D minor, Op. 125 'Choral' (1817-23)

BERLIOZ:
Symphonie fantastique, Op. 14 (1830-1)

BIZET:
Symphony in C (1855)

BRAHMS:
Symphony No. 1 in C minor, Op. 68 (1876)
Symphony No. 2 in D, Op. 73 (1877)
Symphony No. 3 in F, Op. 90 (1883)
Symphony No. 4 in E minor, Op. 98 (1885)

BRITTEN:
Simple symphony for string orchestra, Op. 4 (1933)
Spring symphony (chorus and orchestra) (1949)

BRUCKNER:
Symphony No. 4 in E flat 'Romantic' (1874)
Symphony No. 5 in B flat (1877)
Symphony No. 6 in A (1881)
Symphony No. 7 in E minor (1883)
Symphony No. 8 in C minor (1885)
Symphony No. 9 in D minor (1894)

DVOŘÁK:
Symphony No. 7 in D minor, Op. 70 (1885)
Symphony No. 8 in G, Op. 88 (1889)
Symphony No. 9 in E minor Op. 95 'From the New World' (1893)

ELGAR:
Symphony No. 1 in A flat, Op. 55 (1908)
Symphony No. 2 in E flat, Op. 63 (1910)

FRANCK:
Symphony in D minor (1888)

HAYDN:
Symphony No. 45 in F sharp minor 'Farewell' (1772)
Symphony No. 88 in G 'Letter V' (1787)
Symphony No. 92 in G 'Oxford' (1788)
Symphony No. 94 in G 'Surprise' (1791)
Symphony No. 96 in D (1791)
Symphony No. 99 in E flat (1792)
Symphony No. 100 in G 'Military' (1794)
Symphony No. 101 in D 'Clock' (1794)
Symphony No. 102 in B flat 'Miracle' (1794)
Symphony No. 103 in E flat 'Drum Roll' (1795)
Symphony No. 104 in D 'London' (1795)

MAHLER:
Symphony No. 1 in D 'Titan' (1888)
Symphony No. 2 in C minor 'Resurrection' (1894)
Symphony No. 3 in D minor (1895)
Symphony No. 4 in G (1900)
Symphony No. 5 in C sharp minor (1902)
Symphony No. 6 in A minor (1904)
Symphony No. 7 in E minor (1907)
Symphony No. 8 in E flat (1908)
Symphony No. 9 in D (1909)

MENDELSSOHN:
Symphony No. 3 in A minor, Op. 56 'Scotch' (1841-2)
Symphony No. 4 in A, Op. 90 'Italian' (1833)
Symphony No. 5 in D, Op. 107 'Reformation' (1830/2)

MOZART:
Symphony No. 14 in A, K114 (1771)
Symphony No. 25 in G minor, K183 (1773)
Symphony No. 28 in C, K200 (1773)
Symphony No. 29 in A, K201 (1774)
Symphony No. 31 in D, K297 'Paris' (1778)

MOZART *continued*   Symphony No. 35 in D, K385 'Haffner' (1782)

Symphony No. 36 in C, K425 'Linz' (1783)

Symphony No. 38 in D, K504 'Prague' (1786)

Symphony No. 39 in E flat, K543 (1788)

Symphony No. 40 in G minor, K550 (1788)

Symphony No. 41 in C, K551 'Jupiter' (1788)

NIELSEN: Symphony No. 1 in G minor, Op. 7 (1894)

Symphony No. 3, Op. 27 'Espansiva' (1912)

Symphony No. 4, Op. 29 'Inextin-guishable' (1916)

Symphony No. 5, Op. 50 (1922)

Symphony No. 6 'Sinfonia semplice' (1925)

PROKOFIEV: Symphony No. 1 in D, Op. 25 'Classical' (1917)

Symphony No. 5 in B flat, Op. 100 (1944)

Symphony No. 6 in E minor, Op. 111 (1945)

BENJAMIN BRITTEN (b. 1913) *England*
The great men in art have generally been those who ignored the fashions and simply tried to express their own thoughts and characters most clearly. This is what Benjamin Britten has done. Every note he writes is unmistak-ably his and now we are as used to his musical language as we are to Mozart's and even quite formidable works like his *War Requiem* have been accepted and enjoyed by a very large number of people. His great skill, at which he is unequalled in British music, is in putting words and music together, particularly in operas like *Peter Grimes*. He has done a great service for young music lovers, in introducing them to opera in *Let's Make an Opera*, and to the orchestra in the enjoyable *Young Person's Guide to the Orchestra*.

RACHMANINOV: Symphony No. 1 in D minor, Op. 13 (1895)

Symphony No. 2 in E minor, Op. 27 (1907)

Symphony No. 3 in A minor, Op. 44 (1936)

SAINT-SAËNS: Symphony No. 3 in C minor, Op. 78 (1886)

SCHUBERT: Symphony No. 3 in D, D200 (1815)
Symphony No. 4 in C minor D417 'Tragic' (1816)
Symphony No. 5 in B flat, D485 (1816)
Symphony No. 6 in C, D589 (1818)
Symphony No. 8 in B minor D759 'Unfinished' (1822)
Symphony No. 9 in C, D944 'Great' (1828)

SCHUMANN: Symphony No. 1 in E flat, Op. 38 'Spring' (1841)

Symphony No. 2 in C, Op. 61 (1845-6)

Symphony No. 3 in E flat, Op. 97 'Rhenish' (1850)

Symphony No. 4 in D minor, Op. 120 (1851)

SHOSTAKOVITCH: Symphony No. 1 in F minor, Op. 10 (1925)

Symphony No. 5 in D, Op. 47 (1937)
Symphony No. 6, Op. 54 (1939)
Symphony No. 7, Op. 60 'Leningrad' (1941)

Symphony No. 10 in E minor, Op. 93 (1953)

Symphony No. 11 Op. 103 'Year 1905' (1957)

SHOSTAKOVITCH *continued*	Symphony No. 12, Op. 112 'Year 1917' (1959)		Symphony No. 4 in F minor, Op. 36 (1877) Symphony No. 5 in E minor, Op. 64 (1888) Symphony No. 6 in B minor, Op. 74 'Pathétique' (1893)
SIBELIUS:	Symphony No. 1 in E minor, Op. 38 (1899) Symphony No. 2 in D, Op. 43 (1901) Symphony No. 3 in C, Op. 52 (1907) Symphony No. 4 in A, Op. 63 (1911) Symphony No. 5 in E flat, Op. 82 (1915, revised 1916) Symphony No. 6 in D minor, Op. 104 (1923) Symphony No. 7 in C, Op. 105 (1924)	VAUGHAN WILLIAMS:	Symphony No. 1 'Sea Symphony' (1910) Symphony No. 2 'A London Symphony' (1914, revised 1920) Symphony No. 3 'Pastoral' (1922) Symphony No. 4 in F minor (1935) Symphony No. 5 in D (1943) Symphony No. 6 in E minor (1947) Symphony No. 7 'Sinfonia Antarctica' (1953) Symphony No. 8 (1955) Symphony No. 9 (1958)
STRAVINSKY:	Symphony of Psalms (1930) Symphony in C (1940) Symphony in three movements (1945)		
TCHAIKOVSKY:	Symphony No. 1 in G minor, Op. 13 'Winter Dreams' (1867) Symphony No. 2 in C minor, Op. 17 'Little Russian' (1870) Symphony No. 3 in D, Op. 29 'Polish' (1876)	WALTON:	Symphony No. 1 in B flat (1935) Symphony No. 2 (1960)

INDEX

ACKNOWLEDGEMENTS
Erich Auerbach 8, 85, 86; Austrian National Library 51 top right, 77 top; Barnaby's Picture Library 35 bottom, 49 bottom; Bassano and Vandyck Studios 75 top right, 79 top right; Camera Press Ltd. 79 top left, 91; Connaissance des Arts: P. Millet, R. Guillemot 29 top, 35 top left, 58, 59 bottom; Anthony Crickmay 50-51; Peter Gammond 52; Giraudon 27 top left, 35 top right, 41 right; Will Green 9, 66, 75 top left; Library of Congress, Washington 2, 3, 94, 95; Mansell Collection 11, 17, 33, 37 top, 49 top, 57 top, 61 top, 67, 79 bottom, 81 bottom, 88; F. A. Mella 6-7, 13, 27 top right, 45; National Gallery, London 4; National Portrait Gallery, London 15 top, 19; Novosti Press Agency 87, 89 top; Odhams Syndication Service 40-41;

PAF International 74; Paul Popper Ltd. 55, 65 top, 69 top, 71 top right, 73, 81 top, 83; Radio Times Hulton Picture Library 31, 39 top, 43, 47 bottom right, 53, 59 top, 63 top, 89 bottom; David Redfearn 30, 39 bottom, 80, 74, 77; Royal College of Music and R. B. Fleming 25; Royal Philharmonic Orchestra 46, 47 bottom left; Scala 18 bottom, 21, 23, 47 top; Jim Williams and The Young Music Makers 15 bottom, 16, 18 top, 51 bottom, 54, 56, 57 bottom, 60, 61 bottom, 62, 63 bottom, 65 bottom, 76; Jim Williams 64, 68, 69 bottom, 70, 71 left; Reg Wilson 29 bottom, 37 bottom, 38.
The publishers would like to thank The Young Music Makers for their help in the production of this book.

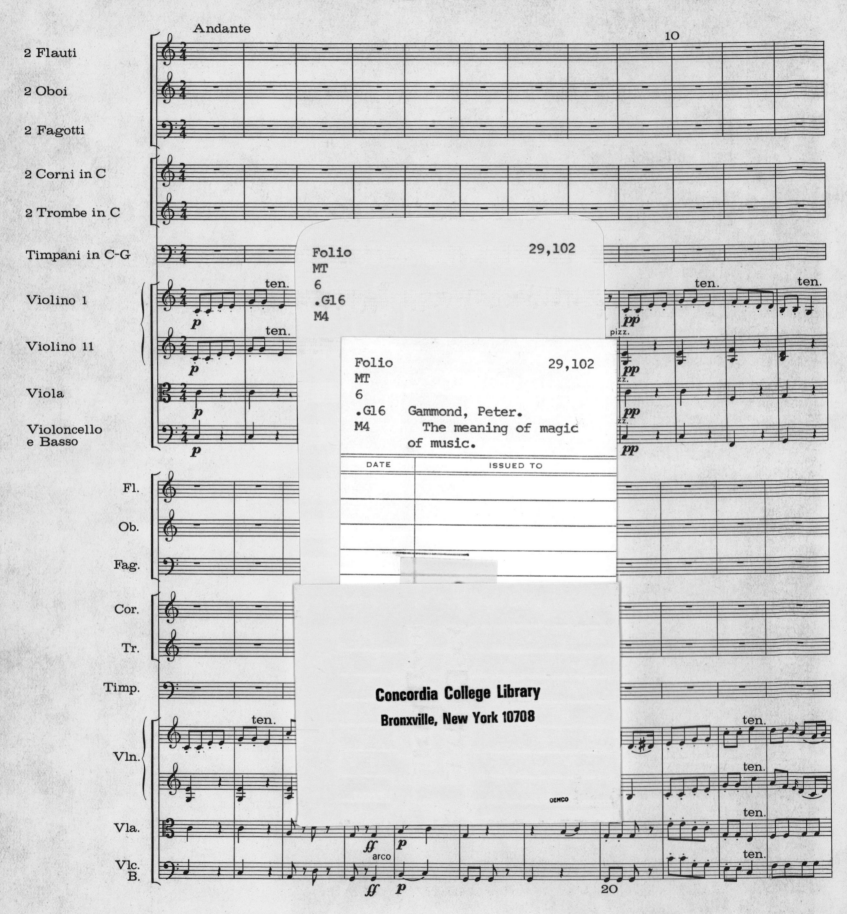